THE ST. ALBANS
—RAID—

THE ST. ALBANS
— RAID —

Confederate Attack on Vermont

MICHELLE ARNOSKY SHERBURNE

THE
History
PRESS

Published by The History Press
Charleston, SC 29403
www.historypress.net

Copyright © 2014 by Michelle Arnosky Sherburne
All rights reserved

Front cover: Original painting of the St. Albans Raid scene on Main Street across from the
Village Green by Robert Eldridge. *Courtesy of Village Frame Shoppe & Gallery, St. Albans, Vermont.*

First published 2014

Manufactured in the United States

ISBN 978.1.62619.629.2

Library of Congress CIP data applied for.

This book is dedicated to my husband, Rodney, and my son, Darren.

CONTENTS

PART III: THE RAIDERS' TRIALS IN CANADA

FOREWORD

The St. Albans Raid is more than a fantastic tale of a New England town taken by surprise by a group of Southerners who robbed the local banks, took people hostage and tried to burn down the town but were chased away by a local posse and captured across the border in Canada. The event took place in the third year of the rebellion and was the northernmost land action of the Civil War.

On the surface, the raid appeared to be the scheme of young renegade Confederate soldiers to rob and plunder an unsuspecting town. In reality, the St. Albans raid was a piece of a larger conspiracy.

In 1863 and 1864, the Confederate government sent agents to Canada to put into motion conspiracy plans against the Federal government and President Abraham Lincoln. The plans included raiding numerous Northern cities, the liberation of Confederate prisoners at Camp Douglas and Johnson's Island and the capture of the USS *Michigan* and steamers *Philo Parsons* and *Island Queen*. The plans also included using Dr. Blackburn's yellow fever and small pox warfare tactics and, the most dreadful conspiracy of all, the assassination of President Lincoln and members of his cabinet.

All of these plans could have had serious repercussions that might have changed the course of American history and, quite possibly, that of Canada and Britain. Raid eyewitness and St. Albans native Edward A. Sowles stated that he spoke directly to Lincoln's secretary of war, Edwin Stanton, who said that the raid was "one of the important events of the War, not so much as transferring in part the scenes and horrors of war to a peaceful, loyal state, but as possibly leading to serious and dangerous complications with Great Britain through the desires and efforts of the Southern people to involve Canada and, through her, Britain in a war on behalf of their Southern friends."

The raid did not go as planned. The raiders fled to Canada, pursued by a St. Albans posse of civilians headed by Captain George P. Conger, of the First Vermont Cavalry, who was home on leave. Fourteen of the twenty-one raiders were seized in Canada over the next couple days, while the other seven escaped. The Americans were asked to surrender their prisoners to the Canadian authorities, which they did. The U.S. government immediately asked for their extradition under the provisions of the Webster-Ashburton Treaty, agreed to in 1842 by the United States and Great Britain.

The Webster-Ashburton Treaty was used primarily to settle a number of serious disputes between the United States and Canada. One of the rules of the treaty, however, specified that suspected criminals arrested for such crimes as robbery, assault and murder on either side of the border were to be returned to the site of the suspected crime for trial. On the other hand, soldiers carrying out their assigned tasks during wartime would be exempt from arrest and prosecution. The fourteen raiders were transferred to Montreal, and months of trials, releases and re-arrests occurred. Eventually, only five raiders remained in custody into 1865.

Great Britain did not support the Confederate states in the war, but it did note that a state of belligerency existed between the Union and the Confederacy. Soldiers on either side carrying out their orders to subdue the opposition would be regarded under the Webster-Ashburton Treaty as merely doing their duty and exempt from prosecution.

So who were the raiders? Vermonters and, indeed, the United States considered them bandits and murderers, noting that there was nothing to indicate otherwise. St. Albans witnesses testified that the raiders shouted repeatedly that they were Confederate soldiers, but they did not wear Confederate uniforms. The arrested men, on the other hand, said they were Confederate soldiers simply carrying out orders. They went through a somewhat lengthy process to prove their status by dispatching three representatives to Richmond, Virginia, to obtain a copy of Bennett Young's orders. Two made it, but the third was captured by Union forces and tried as a spy.

The decision about what to do with the prisoners depended on the Canadian court system. Adding to the problem was the fact that the relationship between the U.S. government and Canada–Great Britain was already strained and had been since the War of 1812.

In that conflict, the United States had declared war because of the impressment of American soldiers by the British. Other issues consisted of British trade restrictions, the support of American Indian tribes against American expansion, the violation of British copyright laws by certain Americans and an argument with Canada over American-Canadian borders. The relationship didn't improve much over the next forty years. During the French Canadian rebellion in 1837–38, defeated French Canadian refugees fled across the border to upper New York State and northern Vermont hoping to continue the fight with the assistance of local anti-British Americans. This support angered the British, who threatened to strike back at the local Americans. The border disputes between the United States and Canada were a major bone of contention. It took a long time and the talents of two superb representatives—U.S. representative Daniel Webster and British negotiator Lord Alexander B. Ashburton, who together created the Webster-Ashburton Treaty of 1842—to provide the basis to help settle these and other disputes.

On April 5, 1865, after several trials over a five-month period, a decision was made that the attack on St. Albans by Lieutenant Young and his associates "must be regarded as a hostile expedition undertaken and carried out under the authority of the so-called Confederate States under the command of one of their officers." Therefore, these acts were not to be dealt with under ordinary criminal law. Montreal Superior Court judge James Smith decided that the prisoners could not be extradited, that he had no jurisdiction over them and that they were entitled to discharge. However, the five men were immediately re-arrested and shipped to Toronto for violation of neutrality laws in Ontario, where the planning for the attack on St. Albans had allegedly taken place.

General Robert E. Lee's Army of Northern Virginia surrendered to General U.S. Grant's army on April 9, 1865. The entire country was thrown into chaos when President Abraham Lincoln was shot on April 14, 1865, and died the following day. The defeat of other Confederate armies continued until the last army surrendered on June 2, 1865, and the war was over. With this, the trial of the five Confederate raiders was terminated, and they were released. They disappeared over time. Many Americans were indignant; they wanted to see the raiders tried in a U.S. court. There was a good chance that the raiders would have been hanged, just as eight U.S. soldiers had been hanged in Georgia in 1862 when they were captured by Confederates after they had seized a Confederate locomotive called "the General."

Although many Americans were disappointed at the time with the outcome of the trial of the raiders in Montreal, looking back today, 150 years later, one can say that the handling of the entire affair worked out well. It avoided war with Canada and Britain and worked to everyone's long-term advantage. It would have been catastrophic if Captain George Conger had refused to turn over his prisoners to the Canadian authorities upon request. And it would have also been catastrophic if the Canadians had merely released the raiders after their arrest rather than conducting trials under the provisions of the Webster-Ashburton Treaty. Another possible catastrophe could have resulted if the U.S. military had followed Major General John Dix's order to cross the Canadian border and arrest or destroy the raiders, as the United States would have faced violating Canadian neutrality laws.

—DONALD MINER

Donald Miner, a native of St. Albans, Vermont, has been a dedicated historian and supporter of the St. Albans Historical Society and Museum since the 1990s. He served as director of the St. Albans Historical Society and Museum for years and is currently a trustee emeritus.

Acknowledgements

I must begin with my deepest gratitude to my husband, Rodney, and my son, Darren, for their love, constant support, encouragement and patience when I delve into researching and "history harvesting" and become consumed in writing. Also to my parents, Jim and Deanna Arnosky, who guide me with their wisdom and encouragement and support me with love.

My utmost gratitude to the St. Albans Historical Society and Museum and its members, including the 150th Commemoration Committee, for their support of this book project and taking time from their hectic sesquicentennial preparation schedule to open their hearts, archives and resources to me. I owe a huge debt of gratitude to Donald Miner, a fountain of knowledge and wealth of history, who has devoted so much time to helping me with this endeavor. You are an inspiration!

My thanks to Alex Lehning for being my liaison at the museum; Charlotte Pedersen and Louise Haynes for your assistance and time in the archives; Robert Eldridge for your incredible painting and graciousness to allow me to use it on the cover; and to all the St. Albanians I pestered with phone calls (because I didn't know anybody in town and had to figure out who to talk to!). Kudos to the St. Albans 150th Raid Committee for the great website and the *St. Albans Messenger* for the great media coverage.

I am forever grateful to Daniel Rush and E. Gale Pewitt for their unbelievable generosity in sharing their knowledge, research, photo collection and beautiful maps with me. Dan and Gale, your research is incredible and thorough, and it came highly recommended. I thank you for your enthusiasm in sharing with a fellow historian.

Thank you to Leonard "Len" Riedel Jr. of the Blue and Gray Education Society for publishing "St. Albans Raiders" and also for putting me in touch with Dan and Gale; to Dudley Pewitt Swiney and Kristin Risinger for your beautiful cartography and prompt response when I needed it; to Dave Allen of www.old-maps.com; to the Vermont Historical Society and Marjorie Strong for your many trips to the vault; to Jeffrey Marshall and the University of Vermont Special Collections Department for your assistance; to Wayne Mitchell for use of his Civil War haversacks; to Dan Pattullo at Village Frame Shoppe in St. Albans; and to Tom Ledoux for his great resources on www.vermontcivilwar.org.

I feel it is important to note the invaluable sources about the history of the St. Albans Raid. Thanks to the diligence and life works of John Branch Sr., Oscar Kinchen and Carl Johnson, information about the raid lives on. The St. Albans Historical Society is responsible for publishing numerous accounts about the raid, which made researching a joy.

I also thank Ken Thomson for allowing me to use the unique Raiders at Niagara Falls photo from his collection and Jim Fouts for his enthusiasm for sharing history and making it come alive in the five-hour walking-driving tour of the raid events in St. Albans. You are fantastic! Deep appreciation to my friend Lorna Renfrew, who was a source of encouragement and went on history quests to Manchester, New Hampshire, to find Elinus and to St. Albans to explore. Also thanks to Rebecca Cummings for sharing in the five-hour tour and your enthusiasm for history and to Lillian "Gay-C" Gahagan for the fun photo shoot.

I am grateful for the patience and support of Connie Sanville of the *Journal Opinion*, who allowed me time to escape from my real job to set up shop to make phone calls, go on history quests, etc.

Thank you to The History Press and my commission editor, Katie Orlando, for going above and beyond in this project on a tight schedule. Thanks also to my project editor, Will Collicott; publicist, Katie Parry; and sales rep, Dani McGrath.

If it wasn't for my faith and God's peace that passes all understanding, I would not have been able to tackle such a huge task in such a short time.

I appreciate the opportunity to share this fascinating Vermont story.

Part I

Setting the Stage

Chapter 1

THE REBELS ARE IN VERMONT!

Far from the battlefields and war zones of the Civil War, New Englanders had the geographic advantage of not experiencing the fear, rampage and invasion that Confederate states did. However, their sons, husbands and fathers were experiencing it, and Northerners in general experienced it vicariously through soldiers' letters, stories and newspaper accounts.

That all changed when the war hit home in Vermont on October 19, 1864. Vermonters were plunged into a state of emergency when St. Albans was held hostage by Confederate soldiers, who robbed three banks, shot citizens and tried to burn the town.

"St. Albans Invaded! Several Citizens Shot! Great Excitement Prevails! Three Banks Robbed! Loss Estimated at about $150,000." Headlines seemed impossible and outlandish in the northern part of Vermont. As the *Vermont Watchman* reported:

> *A party of about twenty-five, armed with revolvers, entered our town this afternoon, stole horses as they chanced to find them in our streets, robbed the several banks of many thousand dollars—some place the sum of $150,000, but there is no chance to get particulars now. Our community is in the greatest excitement. A party has gone in pursuit of the raiders, and the citizens generally are arming themselves as best they can with revolvers, shot guns, &c., and our compositors, partaking of the great excitement, are in arms mostly, and consequently we can say but little of the affair to-day. C.H. Morrison, C.H. Huntington, and one or two others, were shot.*

On October 27, 1864, the *Newport News* reported "that the State had been invaded by land pirates from the neighboring provinces; that the village of St. Albans had been sacked, citizens murdered in cold blood, banks robbed of an immense amount of treasure, and all the crimes of the highwayman, the robber, and the incendiary committed within the borders of our gallant State."

Vermont governor John Gregory Smith was at the statehouse in Montpelier when the following telegraph message came in from St. Albans: "Southern raiders are in town, robbing banks, shooting citizens, and burning houses." His family was in the center of it, living in St. Albans, but Smith put his state first, immediately issuing the order to "stop every train on the railroad…call back that which has just left Montpelier Junction."

Smith put the state of Vermont on high alert and in a state of emergency.

OCTOBER 19 IN THE SOUTH AND IN THE NORTH

In the South, October 19, 1864, would make history. On that day, General Jubal Early's Confederate forces in Shenandoah Valley began the campaign successfully with his troops attacking before daylight and taking Union forces by surprise.

Union general Philip Sheridan was at a meeting in Winchester and away from the frontline when Early launched his early morning attack. The Confederates had the upper hand all day long until General Sheridan rushed to the battle scene and rallied the Union troops. The famous "Sheridan's Ride," with the general charging along Union front lines to inspire his men, is historic. The Union forces beat Early's troops until they surrendered and then took their artillery and supplies.

The Battle of Cedar Creek was a huge victory for the Union troops and the last major battle of the war in the Shenandoah Valley. In this battle, Sheridan's 32,000 Union soldiers faced 11,000–16,000 Confederate soldiers. At the end of the battle, the Confederates' losses totaled 2,910 with a breakdown of 320 killed, 150 wounded and over 1,000 missing. The Union losses were 5,665 casualties consisting of 644 killed, 3,430 wounded and 1,591 missing.

Cedar Creek was one of the war's bloodiest battles and involved nine Vermont regiments, the largest number of Vermont regiments involved in a single battle.

While the Union forces were trouncing General Early's Confederate forces at Cedar Creek, Virginia, St. Albans in Vermont was under attack.

Jeffrey Marshall wrote in *War of the People*, "War against the Union, Vermonters were reminded, meant war on Vermont."

Chapter 2

OUR COUNTRY IN THE MIDST OF THE CIVIL WAR

What was happening in our country in 1864? By the third year of the Civil War, both the Northern and Southern forces were wearing down. The War of the Rebellion, as it was called in the nineteenth century, had been fought in the Southern states with devastation to cities, towns, homes, plantations and industries. The Union was working its way to the capital city of Richmond, Virginia, and the Confederacy was getting nervous.

In September 1864, Union forces led by General William Tecumseh Sherman captured Atlanta, Georgia, and began the forced evacuation of the city. Infamous Confederate raider John H. Morgan, working with depleted forces, was shot in Greeneville, Tennessee, during an attempted attack.

From September to mid-October, Union general Sheridan and Confederate general Early were in what President Lincoln called a deadlock in the Shenandoah Valley. On September 19, Confederate troops were badly beaten at the Battle of Winchester in Virginia. General Sherman and Confederate general John Hood's troops were involved in minor fighting in Georgia into October, with each side trying to gain the upper hand. But the attention was in Virginia, where the Shenandoah Valley campaign was heating up with battle after battle. General Early was working his forces toward Washington to capture the capital and disable the Federal government.

From 1861 to 1863, a prison exchange system was developed by Union major general John A. Dix and Confederate major general D.H. Hill. The "Dix-Hill Cartel of 1862" agreement established a system of equivalent scales based on rank. This worked for a while, but then each side realized that by exchanging prisoners, they were releasing soldiers who would return to fight against them.

But the real demise of the prisoner exchange system was the fact that, in 1863, the Confederacy refused to treat black prisoners the same as whites. President Abraham Lincoln issued a prisoner rule that he would execute a Confederate prisoner of war for every Union prisoner executed, but with blacks not being considered "prisoners" by the Confederates, this posed a problem.

In 1864, the "prisoner gap" gave General Ulysses Grant a decided military advantage. So the exchange system dissolved, which meant that both sides had to construct prison camps. Camps were hastily constructed and not designed for permanent living conditions. There were 150 prisons in the North and South. As the war dragged on, supplies and resources lessened, so prisoners were subjected to horrible living conditions, food shortages and overcrowding.

There were 211,000 Union prisoners and 215,000 Confederate prisoners. By the end of the war, the death toll for prisoners was 10 percent of all Civil War fatalities. In a fourteen-month period at the Confederate Andersonville Prison in Georgia, 13,000 of the 45,000 soldiers imprisoned there died. In the North, at the Union's Elmira Prison in New York, about 13,000 had died, similar to Andersonville.

The Confederacy would attempt major prison liberations to pull soldiers back onto the battlefields.

Chapter 3
CONFEDERATE SECRET SERVICE

The Confederate government, with President Jefferson Davis at the helm, knew it had to try different tactics in 1864 to alleviate the slow-motion domino effect of losses that could eventually lead to the Confederacy's demise. It had to come up with alternative ways to defeat the Union.

The Confederacy focused on behind-the-scenes plans to undermine President Abraham Lincoln and the Federal government and strengthen the Confederate forces. Davis had initially tried to get assistance from overseas. The Confederacy had sent agents to England and other countries in 1863 to rally support for their cause, thinking that an influx of financial support would infuse the Confederate troops with much-needed supplies. But the foreign aid did not materialize because European leaders did not want to risk their relations with the U.S. government by financially supporting the Rebels.

"Despite the failure of our representatives in European countries to rouse apathetic kings and dilly-dallying emperors to come to our aid, it was hard for us to believe that our courage would not be rewarded at length by some powerful succor, or yielding," wrote Virginia Clay-Clopton, wife of Confederate commissioner Clement Clay Jr., in her autobiography, *A Belle of the Fifties: Memoirs of Mrs. Clay of Alabama.*

Support for the Confederacy was found far north in Canada. At the outset of the war, the Canadian government sided with the Confederacy because of major tensions with the U.S. government. It seems ironic that a large exodus of fugitive slaves from the United States found refuge in Canada, yet Canadians were supportive of the Confederacy, which consisted of slave owners. Canada's Confederate sympathies were merely political, as slavery was not allowed there.

As early as 1863, Lincoln's secretary of state, William H. Seward, contacted Canadian officials and the British foreign minister and informed them that the Federal government knew Confederates had found refuge on Canadian soil. The Federal government was aware of the fact that Confederate commissioned officers were headquartered in Canada, and the Lincoln administration saw that as a conflict of interest on the part of both Canada and Great Britain. Also living in Canada were thousands of Confederate prisoners of war who had escaped from Union prisons, as well as insurgents sympathetic with the Confederate cause.

In a December 20, 1863 letter to Honorable Charles Frances Adams, American minister at the Court of St. James, Seward wrote, "In the opinion of this Government, a toleration in Great Britain, or in those provinces, of the practices avowed by the insurgents, after the knowledge of them now communicated to his lordship, would not be neutrality, but would be a permission to the enemies of the United States to make war against them from British shores."

Confederate plans to liberate Southern prisoners in Union prisoners close to the Canadian border were in the works as early as 1863.

From the beginning of the war, the Confederacy had an established secret service division with heavy funding from the Confederate States of America. President Davis approved over $1.5 million in gold for secret service expenditures. During the first two years of the war, approximately $300,000 was spent on secret service endeavors. Approximately $1.2 million was approved for clandestine operations in 1864 and 1865. Funds slated for the St. Albans Raid operation were $100,000.

Davis planned to send commissioners and secret agents to set up headquarters in Canada in order to promote a secret operative that would weaken Northern forces. After receiving their orders, these commissioners would work their way through blockades, sieges and the Northern states to get to Niagara Falls on the Canadian side.

On April 27, 1864, Davis appointed Jacob Thompson, Clement Claiborne Clay and James Holcombe as his commissioners. Because of his experience, George Nicholas Sanders joined their forces as a top operative.

Thompson, a Mississippian, was the former U.S. secretary of the interior; Clay was a former Alabama senator; James Holcombe was a law professor at the University of Virginia; and George Sanders had been involved with the Texas annexation, had served as ambassador to London and had many covert connections.

Confederate commissioner Jacob Thompson, a Mississippian, was the former U.S. secretary of the interior. When the Southern states seceded from the Union, Thompson became part of Jefferson Davis's CSA administration. He was the head commissioner sent to Canada to organize covert operations there. *Public domain.*

Thompson headed to Montreal first and then sent his secretary, William W. Cleary, to Toronto to establish their office at the Queens Hotel. Sanders arrived in Canada from his European stint and went to Toronto.

Clay had been in line for a military appointment, but President Davis instead made him a commissioner to Canada. "Mr. Clay felt it his duty to accept the high responsibility of a diplomatic mission to Canada, with a view to arousing in the public mind of this near-by British territory a sympathy for our cause and country that should induce a suspension of hostilities," wrote Clay-Clopton.

In June, Clay went to Montreal, where he met Holcombe and Thompson, and then headed to Niagara. The mission of the Confederates in Canada was to focus on acts of terrorism that would undermine the Union government and also cause the North to call troops from the South to defend towns and the border. It was hoped that Union reaction would appear to be a breach of neutrality and cause Britain to support Canada and, in turn, the Confederacy.

In *History of the St. Albans Raid*, Edward Sowles wrote that Union generals in the North had been privy to information that "certain leading men of the South" had found their way through the Union lines into the neighboring provinces of Canada, and it was soon ascertained beyond question that Thompson, Clay Jr., Holcombe and Sanders were the accredited agents of the Confederate States in Canada, stationed in Niagara and other important points. Sowles wrote that "the purposes of their mission became very apparent to Mr. Seward and Mr. Stanton, Secretary of War." Washington knew that these commissioners, operating on "neutral territory," had an advantage over the northern frontier of the Union states.

Word spread that the Confederates harbored in Canada were up to no good and to be on guard. General John Dix, in command of the Department of the East, had been notified. Stanton sent a message to British diplomat Lord Richard Lyons in Canada stating, "In the present peaceful aspect of affairs we shall not make any such military demonstrations, or preparations on the Vermont line, as General Dix suggests."

With so much focus on the battles being fought in the Southern states, it was difficult to station large numbers of troops on the northern U.S. border. But Dix kept the northern border states informed.

Interestingly enough, on November 20, 1863, Vermont governor John Gregory Smith sent a request to Washington's War Department for five thousand muskets, a large quantity of ammunition, horses for a battery unit and the authority to station troops at Swanton, St. Albans and Burlington.

In Vermont, an inspection was performed to decide whether it was necessary to station troops on the state's border. In a November 28, 1863 telegraph message to Stanton, Major General Dix wrote, "All is arranged well in Vermont." So the answer to Governor Smith was no.

Chapter 4
CONFEDERATE PEACE PLANS

In Canada, the Confederate commissioners didn't waste any time. The first strategy was an attempt to organize a peace conference in Niagara Falls, New York, with President Lincoln and his administration. The objective was to force Lincoln's hand to say no to peace, which, in turn, would make him look bad for the upcoming 1864 presidential election in the North. The Confederates figured that if the South appeared willing to negotiate peace and Lincoln refused, Northerners, tired of the war's drain, would oust him and get someone fresh to wrap up the war.

George Sanders pushed the peace conference and invited influential Northerners to Niagara Falls. The conference could shed light on Lincoln's growing weakness after three years of war, or it could prove that Lincoln was interested only in winning the war and not in keeping the Union together.

The objective would be to hinder the Lincoln administration by weakening Northern support of the war itself.

Sanders orchestrated the peace conference with the assistance of William "Colorado" Jewett, a peace advocate who had lobbied in Europe for peaceful resolutions to America's Civil War. Jewett was associated with peace advocate Horace Greeley, editor of the *New York Tribune*, and, later, emissary for Lincoln. Greeley became the liaison for the Niagara Confederates and Lincoln.

Jewett wrote the following to Greeley on July 5, 1864: "I am authorized to state to you…that two ambassadors of Davis & Co. are now in Canada, with

George Nicholas Sanders, a Kentuckian, had a notorious reputation during the Civil War. He was a Confederate operative who aided the commissioners in Canada and also took care of the St. Albans raiders when they were imprisoned. *Courtesy of the William Notman Photographic Collection, McCord Museum, N-000.68.1.*

full and complete powers for a peace, and Mr. Sanders requests that you come on immediately to me…He says the whole matter can be consummated by me, you, them, and President Lincoln."

Greeley traveled to Niagara and stayed on the American side of the falls at the International Hotel, while the Confederate commissioners stayed at the Clifton House on the Canadian side. Ultimately, the conference was a lot of hot air that resulted in no power and no peace. In reality, none of the commissioners were authorized by Davis to enter into negotiations with Lincoln. Also, the Confederate directive for peace was negotiable only if Southern independence was the end result. That would not work with the Lincoln administration. Lincoln wrote a response to the peace conference on July 18, 1864, now known as his "To Whom It May Concern" letter. It stated:

> *Any proposition which embraces the restoration of peace, the integrity of the whole Union, and the abandonment of slavery, and which comes by and with an authority that can control the armies now at War against the United States, will be received and considered by the Executive Government of the United States, and will be met by liberal terms on other substantial and collateral points, and the bearer or bearers thereof shall have safe-conduct both ways.*

Despite the appearance of coming to an agreement with the Confederacy, Lincoln saw the conference as a ploy. His response via Greeley was that if the Confederate government wanted to talk peace, it would have to go to Washington.

The commissioners feigned frustration at Lincoln's response, but it was exactly what they had anticipated. Lincoln's "no negotiating" stance sent the message that the Confederacy wanted sent to the war-weary Union. In the November 5, 1864 edition of *Harper's Weekly*, an article about the "Ultimate Convention" quoted Jefferson Davis as saying, "My first effort was for peace…and I sent commissioners to endeavor to arrange an amicable dissolution. From time to time I have repeated efforts to that end, but never, never have I sought it on any other basis than independence." Davis confirmed in the article that Clay and Thompson had no authority to propose peace on the basis of restoration of the Union. The only platform the Confederacy would talk peace on would be that of Southern independence.

"As a result, the peace talks fell through on the excuse that the Confederate commission was not specifically empowered to negotiate a peace," wrote William Tidwell in *Come Retribution*. But the underlying Confederate goal had been accomplished. Lincoln had refused, and that meant bad publicity for Lincoln.

Chapter 5

PEACE DIDN'T WORK—
ON TO PLAN B

The commissioners had a Plan B ready after the failure of the peace conference.

The second scheme was freeing over five thousand Confederate prisoners held at Camp Douglas near Chicago, Illinois. Camp Douglas was notorious for its poor conditions and high death rate; 10 percent of the prison population had died in one winter.

The commissioners had at their disposal a large number of Confederate soldiers who had sought refuge in Canada after escaping war prisons. In *Confederate Operations in Canada*, Confederate lieutenant John Headley, a colleague of Clay, Thompson, Holmes and Sanders, wrote, "Many of these men had escaped from prison under circumstances which illustrated their daring and fertility of resource."

In August 1864, sixty-four commissioned agents were sent from Canada to Chicago on the mission. The officers were Captain Thomas Hines of the Ninth Kentucky Cavalry, Company E, and Major John Breckinridge Castleman of Morgan's Second Kentucky Cavalry. The roster of the August 29 Camp Douglas crew included sixteen of the soon-to-be St. Albans raiders. The agents were issued pistols, an act that was recorded in the Confederate War Records as "Report of the Adjutant General of the State of Kentucky, Kentucky Confederate Volunteers, 1861–1865."

A new recruit who had escaped Camp Douglas was Kentucky cavalryman and former Morgan's Raider Bennett Henderson Young, a twenty-one-year-old on his first Confederate mission. Young had traveled to

Lieutenant Bennett Henderson Young, age twenty-one, was the commander of the Fifth Company of the CSA Retributors and led the St. Albans Raid on October 19, 1864. *Courtesy of the University of Vermont Libraries, Special Collection, Bailey/Howe Library.*

Richmond and had been appointed first lieutenant of a Provisional Army by President Davis and sent to Canada for missions there. In the Confederate War Records, the expense sheet for "Lieut. B.H. Young" records that Clay issued cash to Young on the dates of July 27, August 25, September 8, September 15 and September 30 totaling $642 for operative expenses. Young was on the payroll and had an expense account.

The sixteen would-be St. Albans raiders on the Camp Douglas mission were: Lieutenant Bennett Young, Alamanda Bruce, Joseph Bettersworth, Charles Daniel, James Doty, Samuel Gregg, C.H. Higbee, William H. Huntley, Samuel Lackey, John Mock, Louis Price, Marcus Spurr, Charles Swagar, Squire Tevis, William Tevis and Caleb Wallace.

The day of the planned Camp Douglas attack coincided with the National Democratic Convention. The city was filled with conventioneers, which meant enhanced security and too many civilians to deal with. Also, officials increased the number of Federal guards at Camp Douglas to prevent attacks. Because of these factors, the escape mission was aborted. It was on to Stage 3.

Commissioner Jacob Thompson orchestrated the next prison escape. The plan was to liberate seven thousand prisoners on Johnson's Island in Lake Erie, near Sandusky, Ohio. Thompson worked with John Yates Beall of the Confederate volunteer navy. If the Confederates could capture the Union gunboat USS *Michigan*, they would gain control of the Finger Lakes system and of towns in New York, Ohio, Illinois, Michigan and Wisconsin.

Before the mission, Beall was in Buffalo, New York, and needed funding delivered. New recruit Young volunteered to dispatch the money from Thompson to Beall, taking indirect routes to New York with the help of a network of spies.

Stage 3 was scheduled for September 19, 1864. Confederate agents, under Beall's command, captured the steamer *Philo Parsons* on Lake Erie and then the *Island Queen*. Beall was to sail near Johnson's Island, where the *Michigan* guarded Confederate prisoners. But the plot was discovered, and the prisoner liberation didn't happen.

Beall burned the *Philo Parsons*, so the Union was down only one ship and had not lost its stronghold of the Great Lakes and thousands of Confederate prisoners.

The prisoner liberation attempts close to the Canadian border had failed.

In Canada, the large contingency of Confederates worked together against the Union and were not just hiding out until it was safe to return home to the South.

In Edward Sowles's *History of the St. Albans Raid*, Montreal police chief Guillaume Lamothe was quoted as saying:

> *After the Johnson's Island affair, and before the St. Albans raid, the Southern refugees appeared to be acting together in concert, and to be fully organized in Canada, and their organization, their purpose and intention of committing acts of forcible depredations, rapine and war upon the territory of the United States, must have been known to the Cartier-McDonald* [Sir George E. Cartier, attorney general, and Sir John A. McDonald, prime minister] *government; that if there had been any steps taken by said government of Cartier-McDonald to prevent the same, the said raid on St. Albans might and would have been prevented, and would not have occurred.*

Next Stage of Planning

Retribution raids had been discussed at length by Sanders, Clay, Secretary of War James Seddon and the newly appointed First Lieutenant Bennett Young. Thompson wasn't in favor of the raids, so Clay delayed the mission by sending Young to Ohio for the liberation mission at Camp Chase near Columbus. Young tried to organize a group of soldiers but, after the recent failures, couldn't recruit enough qualified men.

Retribution raids would accomplish a number of goals for the Confederacy. They would draw troops away from war zones in the South and force them to move north to protect the border; cause fear and terror in the people; and serve as retaliation for the raids and destruction by Generals William Sherman and Philip Sheridan in the Shenandoah Valley, Georgia and South Carolina. Robbing the banks would also help replenish depleted coffers of the Confederacy for the war effort and provide extra money for Confederate operating expenses in Canada. It was also hoped that the Federal troops crossing the Canadian border would violate the neutrality laws, which could draw Great Britain into a war with the Federal government. These raids, common during the Civil War, were military operations referred to as "hit-and-run raids" and focused on burning buildings and destroying towns.

Seddon thought Confederate raids were justified, noting, "It is but right that the people of New England and Vermont especially, some of whose

Confederate secretary of war James Seddon was part of Jefferson Davis's staff and was responsible for giving Young his commission as first lieutenant of the Provisional Army. Seddon oversaw the activity of the Confederate commissioners in Canada from Richmond, Virginia. *Public domain.*

officers and troops have been foremost in these excesses and whose people have approved of their course, should have brought to them some of the horrors of warfare."

TIME TO RAID

Finally, Young was ready to do what he had been sent to Canada for—a retribution raid. Young had originally wanted to conduct these raids but was sidetracked by the Confederate commissioners' activities. Seddon had ordered him to visit Burlington and St. Albans and check out the northern border of Vermont.

Young was told by Seddon that it was acceptable to burn the towns after destroying the banks, stores, factories, railway stations and homes.

At the beginning of October, Young was in Montreal and received a memorandum dated October 6, 1864, from Clay stating, "Your suggestions for a raid upon accessible towns in Vermont, commencing with St. Albans, is approved, and you are authorized and required to act in conformity with that suggestion."

Clement Claiborne Clay Jr. was a senator from Alabama before the Civil War and then became a Confederate commissioner to Canada for President Jefferson Davis. He was the mentor of Lieutenant Young and issued orders and financial backing for the St. Albans Raid. *Courtesy of U.S. Senate Historical Office.*

The upcoming raid would be funded by the Confederate government. On the day he received the official order from Clay, Young was issued a St. Catherine's bank check for $1,400 directly from the Confederate Secret Service account controlled by Clay. The funds were for the upcoming St. Albans mission. The day before the raid, on October 18, Young received an additional $420 from Clay.

Chapter 6

WHY ST. ALBANS, VERMONT?

Back in August, the talk of retribution raids was underway with Young, Clay and Secretary of War Seddon. Seddon had issued an order on August 22, 1864, to Young "to reconnoiter the towns along the northern frontier and select the ones most exposed to attack."

At the end of September and the beginning of October 1864, Lieutenant Young returned from his Vermont reconnaissance mission, having traveled to Burlington, St. Albans and along the northern border of Vermont. St. Albans would be the first target, he reported to Clay. Following Seddon's lead, destroying the town would be retaliation for damage done by the Union army in the South, and "St. Albans in flames would clearly be an act of war and not a mere robbery," William Tidwell wrote in *Come Retribution*. St. Albans was to be the first of many raids of New England towns on the Canadian border that the Confederate commissioners had discussed.

Over several trips, Young gathered information about the town's layout, including the location of banks, livery stables and gun stores, and routes out of town. "Three times Young, who had some skill as a topographer and who was a natural woodsman, traveled over the road from the Canadian border to St. Albans," wrote Roland Franklyn Andrews in an article titled "How 'Unpreparedness' Undid St. Albans" and published in the November 16, 1912 issue of *The Outlook* magazine. Andrews continued, "It was on these visits that he established his reputation as a theological student, for he read his Bible so rigorously at the American House that some of the elderly lady

Bennett Young stayed in the Tremont Hotel (right) while in St. Albans. On the left-hand side beyond the lamppost is the location in front of Miss Beattie's Millinery Shop where Elinus Morrison was fatally shot. *Courtesy of St. Albans Historical Society and Museum.*

boarders considered the propriety of asking him to supply the pulpit at the Congregational Church."

Only about twenty miles from the Canadian border, St. Albans was a perfect target. In the 1860s, St. Albans had developed into a commercial center with the coming of the railroad. Known as "Rail City," St. Albans was the railroad center between New York and Montreal. It was also the headquarters of the Vermont Central Railroad Company and a thriving railcar industry building railcars on site to keep up with the country's demand. Because of the railroad, the town was easily accessible, and there was the added benefit that it sat on St. Albans Bay in Lake Champlain, making lake travel an option as well.

St. Albans served as the shire town serving as the county seat of Franklin County. It was a bustling city, home to county courts, four banks and the market center. In the nineteenth century, farmers' products were shipped out of St. Albans to the rest of New England.

An overview of the Towers, Governor John Gregory and Ann Smith's estate that overlooked the village of St. Albans. *Courtesy of the University of Vermont Libraries, Special Collections, Bailey/ Howe Library.*

In the 1800s, there were 217,000 head of cows in Vermont, and approximately 29,500 were in Franklin County. The annual production of butter in the state of Vermont was 25.0 million pounds, with Franklin County producing 4.5 million pounds of that. Butter buyers traveled from New York, Boston, New Hampshire and within the state to St. Albans for this product alone. Once a week, Market Day—or Butter Day, as the locals called it—was held. That meant the four banks would be handling many large deposits after the end of the day's sales. This regular weekly event also meant a regular influx of strangers. While scouting the town, Young noted that St. Albans had approximately four thousand residents, who were used to having strangers in town. They wouldn't suspect twenty strangers coming to town on business or vacation.

The village layout was perfect for a controlled attack and hostage situation, with the business district about two miles long and only a half mile wide with a large village green on one border. It was unprotected and geographically far enough away from Burlington and the state capital of Montpelier. It was also close to Canada for the raiders' escape and necessary diplomatic sanctuary.

Interestingly enough, since 1863, the threat of raids or attacks were in the works across the Canadian border by the Confederate Secret Service.

Washington was well aware of the threat but focused its energies and protection on the battlefront.

Vermont governor John G. Smith's request to Washington's War Department back in November 1863 for muskets, ammunition and horses would have provided St. Albans with its own protection. In hindsight, Washington should have accepted Smith's request.

On his scouting trips, Young visited Governor Smith's residence and estate, called the Towers. He met the governor's wife, Ann Brainerd Smith, who gave him a tour of the estate and horse stables. The fact that the governor's residence was in the town was a bonus.

Young decided that the raiders would first target Governor Smith's estate to be burned in retaliation for the Union troops burning the home of Virginia governor John Letcher.

Chapter 7

INTRICATE PLANNING FOR THE "VAIRMONT YANKEE SCARE PARTY"

Lieutenant Young had been recruiting and planning for retribution raids throughout the summer of 1864, even while involved with the Confederate prison camp attempts. He called his raid unit the "Fifth Co. C.S.A. Retributors" and had submitted a muster roll to the CSA in August 1864. Some of the documents of muster rolls, expense sheets and petitions pertaining to Young's mission were questioned from the start because they were not available at the start of the St. Albans Raid trial in Montreal on October 27, 1864. It was suspected that the documentation was fabricated and submitted in the February trial in 1865 to cover the Confederate soldiers. But there are enough cross-references, letters and facts to show that Young's unit was formed under the authorization of the Confederate government and in the works as early as August 1864.

At the time of the trials, it was thought that Young and his raiders acted as common criminals for personal gain, and the evidence of a highly structured secret service for the CSA was not known. As time progressed and revealed more information about the Confederacy, the St. Albans Raid was seen in accurate light, just as details of John Wilkes Booth's assassination of President Lincoln took years to be understood.

Young submitted a revised muster roll while in Chicago to Confederate adjutant general Samuel Cooper in an August 31, 1864 letter. "Muster Roll of the 5th Company Confederate States of America Retributors, Lt. Young Commanding at Chicago, Illinois, Dated August 31, 1864" lists the soldiers involved (along with three extra men who didn't participate) in the St. Albans Raid.

A copy of the Confederate expense voucher for the St. Albans Raid was printed in the January 1902 issue of *The Vermonter* magazine along with an article titled "Secret History of the St. Albans Raid" by "Col. Bennett H. Young." *Public domain.*

Young originally planned to recruit thirty soldiers but was ordered to reduce the number to twenty-three. That number had dropped to twenty by the actual raid.

The muster roll lists the names of the soldiers along with their rank, cavalry, company unit, company commander and last status in the States (the majority were former prisoners of war who had escaped). For example, "Thomas Bronsdon Collins, Capt. Co. F, 7th KY Cavalry, Col. D.W. Cheneault, Morgan's Division. Cut off at Cynthiana [Kentucky, June 12, 1864]" or "J.A. Doty, Co. A, 6th KY Cavalry, Col. Grigsby, Escaped from Camp Douglas."

The majority of his crew were fellow Kentuckians, soldiers with whom Young had served under General Morgan. He chose comrades with whom he was familiar and whose strengths and weaknesses he knew. A total of sixteen had escaped from Union prisons, with ten having been prisoners with Young at Camp Douglas. Most of them were in the same situation as Young—stuck in Canada when they wanted to be back at the front. All but Joseph McGrorty, thirty-eight, and William Hutchinson Huntley, thirty-seven, were in their twenties.

Young and his men jokingly referred to the raid as the "Vairmont Yankee Scare Party." The following soldiers became the St. Albans raiders: Thomas Bronsdon Collins, William Hutchinson Huntley, Dudley Moore, Squire Turner Tevis, James Alexander Doty, Alamanda Pope Bruce, Louis Singleton Price, William Thomas Tevis, Samuel Eugene Lackey, George Scott, Marcus Antonius Spurr, Caleb McDowall Wallace, Charles Moore Swagar, Joseph McGrorty, Samuel Simpson Gregg, Charles Higbee and John Moss. The majority of the Retributors also were scheduled for the Camp Douglas and Johnson's Island missions with Young.

In preparation for the upcoming St. Albans Raid, Young had his men relocate to St. Johns, Quebec, so that they could be closer to Vermont. But they were careful not to cross into the United States or set up a base there because that was "enemy territory," and if caught, they could be hanged.

Young had assembled his unit and had completed his fact-finding mission. Now it was time to work out the details of the raid. During the reconnaissance, Young realized that the St. Albans rail yard and St. Albans Foundry Co. employed over five hundred men. The rail yard for the Central Vermont Railway had twenty-three sets of tracks. Not only was it a hub for this new transportation, but St. Albans also manufactured rail cars, so there were car shops, paint shops and passenger car buildings in addition to the large roundhouse and train shed. Employed at the massive rail yard were painters, welders, machinists, track repairmen, engineers, firefighters, brakemen, conductors, dispatchers, porters, flagmen, office staff and many more. He would have to make sure that the rail yard and foundry workers

were kept in the dark during the raid itself.

The Retributors didn't plan on marching into town or ambushing. This would not be like raids with General Morgan and his cavalry soldiers. This Northern terrorist raid would catch unarmed residents off guard, using the element of surprise to the fullest. Young had to plan for everything to be "portable" because the raiders had to carry what they needed, no wagons or horses. They had to find access to transportation and thus raid the livery stables, etc. The key was to discreetly infiltrate the community.

Top: Samuel Eugene Lackey was in Company B of the Sixth Kentucky Calvary and assigned to the scheduled August 29, 1864 attack on Camp Douglas. He was twenty-three when the raid occurred, and he was one of the raiders who later escaped from prison and fled to the States. *Courtesy of St. Albans Historical Society and Museum.*

Left: Thomas Bronsdon Collins was a captain of Company F, Seventh Kentucky Cavalry, and, like Young, a member of Morgan's Raiders. On June 12, 1864, he was cut off from his unit during a skirmish. The twenty-two-year-old was arrested after the St. Albans Raid but escaped after the first release and before the second arrest. It was reported that he and three other raiders escaped down the St. Lawrence and then traveled to Europe. Collins later became a physician and lived in both Belgium and Paris before dying young in 1869. *Courtesy of St. Albans Historical Society and Museum.*

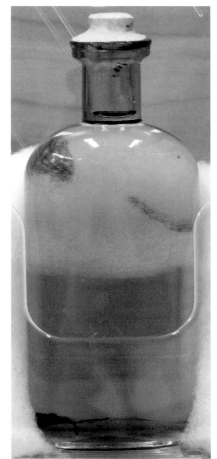

Above: In the collection of the St. Albans Historical Museum is this .36-caliber Colt Navy revolver, the weapon carried by the St. Albans raiders. *Courtesy of St. Albans Historical Society and Museum. Photo by Michelle Arnosky Sherburne.*

Left: A bottle of the incendiary concoction known as Greek fire similar to the ones used by the raiders to start fires throughout town. The concoction, developed in the early centuries by Byzantines, was made from sulfur, naphtha and quicklime. *Courtesy of St. Albans Historical Society and Museum. Photo by Michelle Arnosky Sherburne.*

The weapon of choice was the .36-caliber Colt Navy revolver, a gun commonly issued to cavalry soldiers and carried in saddle holsters. It was a lightweight gun, great for handling, and had a six-round cylinder. Young's raiders were given two revolvers and extra cylinders and ammunition.

Young had decided to use Greek fire and had obtained forty four-ounce flasks, which were distributed prior to the raid. Greek fire was introduced in the seventh century by the Byzantine Greeks. This incendiary material's components had been kept secret for a long time, but the basis of the ingredients are sulfur, naphtha and quicklime. It is a liquid substance that was usually put into a projectile and ignited on contact. This liquid fire cannot be extinguished by water; actually, it flares up more when water is applied. It had been used in warfare through the centuries.

Since the raiders arrived in St. Albans by rail or carriage, the transportation portion of the plan was to round up available horses in St. Albans's livery stables and steal them from townspeople. The plan was to befriend the members of the community and pretend they were Northerners visiting St. Albans. The raid would totally take the town by surprise because no one would suspect the nice, polite, interesting young men who were in St. Albans on vacation or scoping out the business interests.

As Roland Franklyn Andrews wrote in *The Outlook*: "It does not appear that St. Albans noticed anything peculiar in the arrival of twenty boyish strangers, each of whom carried a satchel of a uniform type slung over his shoulder…but how could St. Albans associate a war a thousand miles away with twenty satchels? The boys wandered about the streets, joked with the merchants…"

The element of surprise and ultimate deception would be that they seemed to be "friendlies," but in reality, they were foes waiting to strike like rattlesnakes.

Chapter 8

WHO WAS THIS LIEUTENANT
BENNETT YOUNG?

Young was born in Nicholasville, Kentucky, in 1843 and raised by wealthy and devout Presbyterian parents. His father owned a prosperous hat factory and a large plantation. Young was pursuing his education when the war broke out. In 1863, Young enlisted as a private in the Eighth Kentucky Cavalry unit, which was part of Brigadier General John Hunt Morgan's troops.

The nature of the cavalry unit was unique, and the soldiers were more accustomed to raiding than infantry soldiers. Years after the Civil War, Lieutenant Young wrote in *Confederate Wizards of the Saddle* that cavalry soldiers were required "not only to serve as scouts, but to act as infantry, to cover military movements, to destroy the lines of communication, to burn stores, to tear up lines of railway, to gather supplies, to fight gunboats, capture transports; all these without any equipment of any kind, except their horses, their arms and some horse artillery of limited range."

Young's soldiering experience was molded by his service under Morgan. He and the other cavalrymen were accustomed to raids and destroying railroad and supply routes. In Morgan's troops, only commissioned officers wore uniforms, while the enlistees wore citizens' clothing. The fact that the St. Albans raiders were not in uniform was an important argument in the trials, but these former Morgan's Raiders weren't accustomed to being in uniforms.

Morgan's Raiders were notorious for their bravery and conquering spirits. They were the nemeses of Union troops in Kentucky, Tennessee, Indiana and Ohio. Morgan had over three thousand cavalry soldiers under his command. He and his men terrorized residents, conquered and occupied fifty-two towns, destroyed thirty-four bridges and damaged public and private property. They were responsible for capturing over six thousand Union soldiers and also fought skirmishes and battles.

Oscar Kinchen, in *General Bennett H. Young*, noted that Morgan's Raiders were notorious and that as they moved through Indiana, "residents along the way fled in terror from their homes, leaving open doors and unlocked larders, to seek refuge in the woods and thickets in the neighboring hills." Along their marches, the raiders foraged and took whatever they wanted, with no strategy or method used. Kinchen likened them to boys robbing an orchard. Their reputation as horse thieves preceded them, and people thought they were devils. Morgan's men had to deal with snipers both in the forests and on roadsides, and they became "wanted" men targeted for capture.

Young was in the advance guard of Morgan's cavalry and part of his famous final mission, the Indiana-Ohio Raid of July 1863. That raid "made history as being the longest cavalry raid of the war, with Morgan and his men traveling 700 miles in twenty-five days of almost constant combat against Federal and local state militia units," wrote Russ A. Pritchard in *Raiders of the Civil War: Untold Stories of Actions Behind the Lines*. Over one thousand raiders were captured on July 19, 1863, including General Morgan, Young and future St. Albans raiders. The prisoners were taken to Ohio State Penitentiary in Columbus. In November 1863, Morgan and a small faction of his men tunneled out and escaped. Morgan was killed in action a year later in Tennessee.

Young and fellow Morgan's Raiders were imprisoned first at the state penitentiary and then moved to Camp Chase, west of Columbus, and eventually to Chicago's Camp Douglas. Young spent about six months in prison. After one failed escape attempt, he was sentenced to an underground dungeon for thirty days. However, he was determined and succeeded in his second escape attempt, fleeing to Canada. By the beginning of 1864, Young was living in Toronto and had enrolled in the University of Toronto.

A majority of escaped Confederate prisoners of war were refugees in Canada. Most were waiting for opportunities to return to Confederate service and safely return South, having to work through blockades without getting captured. Knowing that Young and his fellow St. Albans raiders all had similar military experience and had been part of Morgan's Raiders does explain some of the wild and unorthodox soldiering methods found in the group of twenty-one St. Albans raiders.

By the spring of 1864, Young was ready to get back into service for his country. Working his way south, Young had to circumvent the war zones by traveling safely to Halifax, Nova Scotia, and then on to Bermuda, where he would take a ship to the Confederate capital in Richmond, Virginia. Young met one of the Confederate commissioners, Clement Clay, on his way to Canada. This meeting set in motion a series of important events for the Confederacy and for Young. Clay had been ordered by Confederate president Jefferson Davis to help with the secret service missions in Canada along with Jacob Thompson.

Part II

The Raid

Chapter 9

Infiltrating St. Albans

In mid-October, Lieutenant Bennett Young and his twenty soldiers unobtrusively arrived in St. Albans. They traveled by railroad from Montreal and St. Johns in Quebec and via carriages from Burlington. Young and two men arrived on October 10 and checked into the Tremont Hotel. Over the next eight days, small groups of two or three men arrived and registered at the St. Albans House, the American House, the Willard boardinghouse and the Tremont. They made sure not to draw attention to themselves, dropping their southern accents and trying to blend in. The men posed as hunters, horse traders, fishermen, tourists and invalids in Vermont on business and pleasure. The small groups circulated St. Albans and visited with locals. They were friendly, well mannered and neatly dressed. They were careful not to interact with the other raiders because they didn't want to raise suspicions.

The men investigated all the livery stable locations and other places horses were kept around Main Street. Some inquired at shops about purchasing guns for their upcoming hunting expeditions. They even asked about borrowing weapons from residents but learned that locals were not heavily armed.

Originally, Young had chosen October 18 as the day of the raid. But in talking with people, he learned that October 18 was a Tuesday, and in St. Albans, that meant Market Day, or Butter Day, as the locals called it.

In *Advantages, Resources and Attractions of St. Albans, Vt.*, it is stated that on Market Day, the "streets are…thronged with people from the county towns. As many as 300 teams are frequently seen standing in the streets." Teams of farmers from northern Vermont and merchants from all over New England traveled to St. Albans on a weekly basis to sell their wares on Market Day. This posed a problem, as there would be too many people to have to control. Young changed the date of the raid to Wednesday, October 19, when the town would be back to normal.

It had been raining for an extensive period of time, and the roads were muddy and rutted. It had rained overnight on Tuesday, and by Wednesday morning, it was cloudy, gray and wet—a good day to stay indoors. In a letter to a relative, St. Albans resident Susan Hubbell Seymour described October 19 in the following way: "Such mud! Such roads! Such drizzling rain."

Another thing that benefitted the raiders' plan was that on October 19, forty prominent businessmen in St. Albans would be going to Burlington to await decisions on lawsuits in the Supreme Court. Local legislators were in Montpelier, and county sheriff Renesselaer R. Sherman was also in Burlington for the day.

Young had also taken into account the fact that the banks would be easier to rob with fewer customers. Thus, it was decided to hit the banks at 3:00 p.m., close to closing time. The bank employees would still be there to open vaults, so no explosives were necessary.

From his reconnaissance trips, Young was aware of the potential dangers of having the employees of the St. Albans Foundry Co. and the rail yard so close to the "raid scene." So the plan was to station guards at the top of the two streets that led to Main Street, the Village Green and the location of the three banks scheduled to be hit.

Despite the orders and original plans discussed by Young and the Confederate commissioners, robbing the banks was not a last-minute, spontaneous addition to the raid. The original orders and main focus were to burn the town. It had been spelled out by Clay, Thompson and Seddon that the destruction of St. Albans was paramount, not robbing banks.

After the fact, the commissioners and other Confederate officials stressed that the orders issued had not been followed. The viewpoint that the raid was considered a failure was due to the fact that the Confederate commissioners had wanted the town destroyed.

St. Albans lawyer and author Edward Sowles wrote about his conversation with one of the raiders in regards to the original plan, which was to burn the Smith residence as a diversion, thus enabling the raiders to rob the banks while the citizens were fighting the fire, or multiple fires, in town.

Reviewing what has been written about the raid, the order of events and the testimonies during the trials, it is apparent that Young had his own agenda, and burning down the town was not the first on item on it. From all accounts, the first order of raid business was for the teams to hit the banks simultaneously. The banks were to be robbed close to closing time, and the other raiders were to take townspeople hostage and keep the crime scenes quiet. The third order of business was to steal horses.

Yes, the raiders did use the Greek fire, but they used it sporadically. It seemed as if they used it as they were leaving and that burning the town down was not the first order of business.

If burning buildings was the target of the raid, then why did Young choose to use such a small amount of incendiary material? And why were the buildings not torched from the start and then the banks robbed?

There were no reports of any livery stables, hotels or stores along Main Street being set ablaze. The original plan of burning the governor's estate didn't happen. The raiders didn't even go up to the Towers during the raid. Possibly their youth and inexperience got the best of them. Obviously, Young had chosen his own course of action.

Chapter 10

WEDNESDAY, OCTOBER 19, 3:00 P.M.

Wednesday afternoon, after the raiders had enjoyed their noontime meal, it was time for their rendezvous. They met in Young's room at the Tremont Hotel to go over last-minute particulars. They armed themselves with their Colt Navy revolvers and bottles of Greek fire. Extra bullet cylinders were distributed, and the men put them in their haversacks (otherwise known as Moroccan satchels).

Twelve men were to rob the banks, four to round up horses, one to guard the hostages kept on Green and three to guard the streets leading down to the Foundry and rail yard. Young would supervise the action and sound alarm if necessary.

They were ready. The soldiers filtered out of the hotel. It was reported after the raid that a bottle of Greek fire was thrown into the washroom by Thomas Collins but that it didn't burst into flames and only smoldered. Maybe that was a premonition that that Greek fire wasn't going to work.

The soldiers got into position. Checking the time, they found it was almost 3:00 p.m.

Lieutenant Bennett Young exited the Tremont Hotel and walked down the street to the American Hotel. He fired shots in the air to signal the start of the "Vairmont Yankee Scare Party." He turned to several men on the hotel porch and stated, "I am an officer of the Confederate service who is going to take the town!...I take possession of this town in the name of the Confederate States of America!" A written copy of his proclamation was later reportedly found on the sidewalk in front of the American Hotel.

The raiders carried haversacks or Moroccan satchels during the raid to hold their extra cylinders and bottles of Greek fire. This is a replica of a Union army haversack that was commonly used by men on both sides to carry essentials such as eating utensils, Bibles, journals, rations, playing cards, etc. *Courtesy of Wayne Mitchell Civil War Collection. Photo by Michelle Arnosky Sherburne.*

Left: Charles Moore Swagar, First Kentucky Cavalry, Company A, was scheduled to partake in the Camp Douglas attack. After the trials and the Civil War, Swagar went to Europe and fought in the Franco-Prussian War of 1871 and was killed in Paris. *Courtesy of St. Albans Historical Society and Museum.*

Below: The tenth image of *Frank Leslie's Illustrated News*' depiction of the St. Albans Raid shows raiders demanding money from bank teller at the St. Albans Bank. *Courtesy of Michelle Arnosky Sherburne.*

At the top of Champlain and Kingman Streets, raiders George Scott, Charles Swagar and a third unnamed raider, stationed themselves to stop any traffic from going onto Main Street. More importantly, these streets led to the foundry and rail yard.

The targeted banks were First National Bank on Fairfield Street, St. Albans Bank on the corner of Kingman and Main Streets and Franklin County Bank on Main Street, next door to the American House.

The raid began.

At the First National Bank, raiders Caleb Wallace, James Doty, Alamanda Bruce and Joseph McGrorty entered. Wallace approached the counter, pulled out his revolver and said to cashier Albert Sowles, "If you offer any resistance, I will shoot you dead. You are my prisoner."

Wallace held Sowles at gunpoint while Doty, Bruce and McGrorty went into the bank vault and filled their haversacks with bank notes. There were bags on the floor that Sowles told the raiders were full of cents. McGrorty cut a few open to find pennies, just as Sowles had said. The raiders left the bags, but what they didn't know was that one of them was filled with gold.

Eighty-year-old General John Nason had been present for throughout the robbery. A very deaf Nason simply read the newspaper and kept quiet after he saw the guns. The raiders seemed to have left the old man alone.

As they marched Sowles out the door, the men met St. Albans resident William H. Blaisdell, who was told the bank was being robbed. Blaisdell confronted Wallace on the bank steps, and the two began to fight. Blaisdell knocked him down and jumped on him. The fight ended suddenly when McGrorty shoved his revolver into Blaisdell's head. Blaisdell and Wallace were escorted to the Village Green.

On the Village Green, raider Samuel Lackey was guarding hostages at gunpoint. Any residents who were on Main Street or ventured onto the scene were forced to the Green across from the American Hotel. The streets were quiet, but the raiders wanted it to remain that way. Young didn't want the foundry and rail yard workers to be alerted. Containing the raid to Main Street meant keeping everything quiet. It worked—for a while.

Collins Huntington had just left his jewelry store to pick up his children at school when he walked by the Franklin Bank. A stranger came up to him and ordered him to go to the Village Green, but Huntington wasn't aware of what was going on, so he ignored him, thinking the stranger had been drinking. That stranger was Lieutenant Young, who then shot Huntington in the back near the spine, leaving wound along his ribcage. Huntington was assisted to the Green, where other hostages attended to him. He did recover.

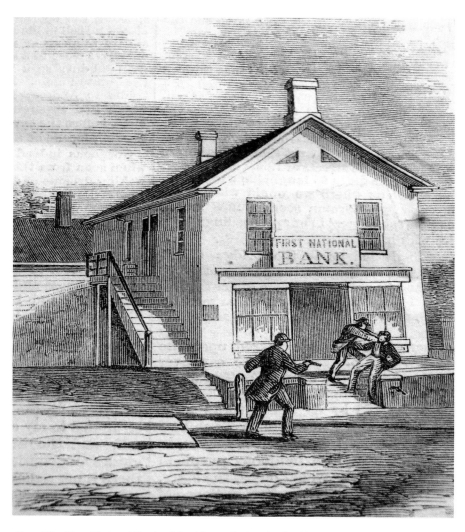

Above: The First National Bank of St. Albans during the St. Albans Raid, as depicted in the November 12, 1864 *Frank Leslie's Illustrated Newspaper* illustration by W.T. Crane. In the illustration, St. Albans resident William Blaisdell assaults one of the raiders to stop the bank robbery while another raider approaches with a gun. *Courtesy of Michelle Arnosky Sherburne.*

Opposite, top: The Village Green was the site of the hostage center during the St. Albans Raid and is depicted in the eighth image of the November 12, 1864 *Frank Leslie Illustrated Newspaper. Courtesy of Michelle Arnosky Sherburne.*

Opposite, bottom: The fifth image of the *Frank Leslie's Illustrated Newspaper's* St. Albans Raid treatment depicts the exterior of the St. Albans Bank, the third target of the raid. *Courtesy of Michelle Arnosky Sherburne.*

Louis Singleton Price served in Company B, Eighth Kentucky Calvary, and was a member of Morgan's Raiders. He was captured and served time at Camp Douglas but escaped. Price was twenty-two at the time of the raid. He died in 1866 when a man chastising him about the raid shot him on the street. *Courtesy of St. Albans Historical Society and Museum.*

At this time, raiders Thomas Collins, Marcus Spurr, Louis Price and Squire Tevis entered St. Albans Bank. Teller Cyrus Bishop rushed to the office to alert Martin Seymour. Seymour and Bishop tried to block the inner door, but the raiders struck Bishop in the forehead and stated, "We are Confederate soldiers detailed from General Early's army to come north and to rob and plunder as your soldiers are doing in the Shenandoah Valley."

From his store next door, Samuel Breck headed to the bank to pay off a note but found that the door was locked. He knocked, and a raider opened the door with a gun aimed at Breck. The raider stole $393 from Breck's hand while Breck protested. Then, a second bank customer, seventeen-year-old Morris Roach, knocked on the door. The raiders allowed him to enter and then stole his $210.

The raiders then went back to Bishop and started questioning him about gold on the premises. Bishop refused to answer until Spurr threatened to put a bullet in his head if he didn't cooperate. Bishop acquiesced and showed

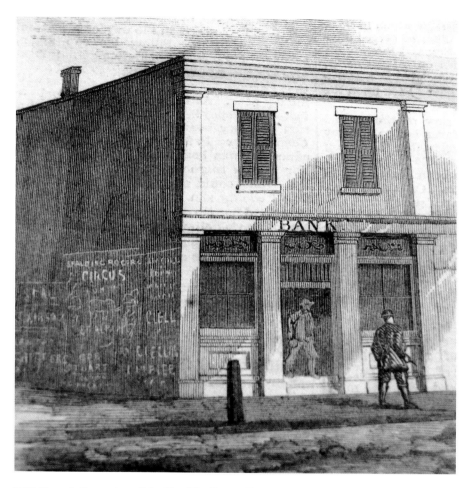

W.T. Crane's illustration of the Franklin County Bank during the St. Albans Raid was the first image appearing in the *Frank Leslie's Illustrated Newspaper*'s segment on the raid. *Courtesy of Michelle Arnosky Sherburne.*

them the sacks of silver in the vault. The raiders took some of the silver but couldn't take them all because they were too heavy. Instead, they filled their haversacks and pockets with silver and bank notes.

Collins forced the four men present to swear allegiance to the Confederate States of America and not shoot the raiders or report the robbery until after they had left. The raiders then exited the bank. They hadn't noticed a pile of paper sheets that looked like wallpaper panels on one of the bank tables. That "wallpaper" was actually freshly printed bank

William Hutchinson Huntley was thirty-seven at the time of the raid. Originally an ordnance expert in Company H, Fourth Georgia Infantry, he was transferred to the Second Georgia Cavalry on special orders. *Courtesy of St. Albans Historical Society and Museum.*

Left: St. Albans wood sawyer Jackson Clark was held prisoner in the Franklin County Bank vault with bank cashier Marcus Beardsley during the St. Albans Raid. *Courtesy of St. Albans Historical Society and Museum.*

Below: This is the actual key that was left in the lock of the Franklin County Bank vault by the raiders. *Courtesy of St. Albans Historical Society and Museum. Photo by Michelle Arnosky Sherburne.*

notes that hadn't been signed or cut yet. It was claimed that $50,000 in uncut bills was passed over. They also left a bag of gold pieces in the vault, not realizing that not all the bags were full of pennies. After the raid, it was reported by Bishop, Seymour, Breck and Roach that these raiders smelled like alcohol.

The third bank to be hit was Franklin County Bank, which raider William Hutchinson entered quietly. There were two customers, James Saxe and Jackson Clark, sitting by a woodstove when he entered, and James Armington was at the teller's window. Hutchinson asked bank cashier Marcus Beardsley about the price of gold. Beardsley then referred him to customer Armington. Hutchinson continued the ruse and bought some gold off Armington, who then left with Saxe. Then, Daniel Butterworth, William Moore and John Moss walked into the bank, drew their revolvers and stated that there were hundreds of Confederate soldiers surrounding the town and planning to burn it down.

Hutchinson then told cashier Beardsley: "We have come to rob your banks and burn your town, and we are going to do it." Hutchinson held two revolvers at Beardsley's head and forced him and customer Jackson Clark, a wood sawyer, into the bank vault. Beardsley pleaded with the raiders not to leave them in the locked vault because they would burn to death if the bank were torched. The raiders left them in the vault, screaming for help, but left the key in the lock. After about twenty minutes, Armington and another man, Dana Bailey, ran into the bank and heard the screams of Beardsley and Clark. They found the key in the lock and freed the men. Meanwhile, Young patrolled Main Street, directed his soldiers and ordered people to the Green.

While the robberies were underway, other raiders were ordered to round up horses. Horses were taken from the William and Erasmus Fuller Stables behind Tremont Hotel, from Field's Livery Stable on Champlain Street and from Dennis Gilmore's stable on Champlain Street. In addition, nine horses were cut from wagons, carriages and hitching posts, and one was stolen directly from a bystander.

Raider Charles Higbee was in Field's Livery Stable stealing horses when stable owner Sylvester Field tried to stop him. Higbee shot at him, and the bullet passed through Field's stovepipe hat. Higbee left with the horses. Other raiders entered stores and stole saddles, bridles and blankets.

Lorenzo Bingham's horse was hitched just north of the Franklin Bank, and he was returning to it when he spotted a raider getting on it. Bingham ran toward him and tried to knock the raider off his horse. He was shot at,

The illustration of St. Albans's Main Street in the November 12, 1864 edition of *Frank Leslie's Illustrated Newspaper* shows the raiders seizing horses from farmers' wagons. *Courtesy of Michelle Arnosky Sherburne.*

and the raider took off. As it turned out, Bingham was saved by his silver watch. Years later, his daughter Lizzie Bingham wrote that her father "got hit with a bullet but [was] not hurt. He was standing at the point where the bank near the American Hotel is now. A stray bullet side glanced, struck a heavy silver watch he was wearing and fell to the sidewalk…Shortly after Father came walking in with only a graze on his belly just in front of his hip bone."

Erasmus Fuller returned to St. Albans from a business trip in time to see chaos on Main Street and strangers taking seven horses from his stables. Fuller testified at the Morrison inquest on October 21, 1864, that he had been "passing south on the east side of Main Street and saw a band of men on horseback arrive with pistols coming north on said Main Street. I heard and saw said horsemen firing pistols coming north on Main Street. I saw armed men taking horses that were hitched in front of the stores and leading and riding horses from my stable on the opposite side of said Main Street." He began yelling at the raiders, who warned him they would shoot him. Fuller pulled a six-shooter and tried to shoot, but it failed. Young, who was right there, laughed at the sad defense attempt and then ordered Fuller to go into Bedard's Harness Shop for spurs.

Fuller ran into the harness shop to try to repair his gun, but he gave up and ran out the back door. He then ran to the construction site of the future two-hundred-room, five-store Welden House at the corner of Bank Street

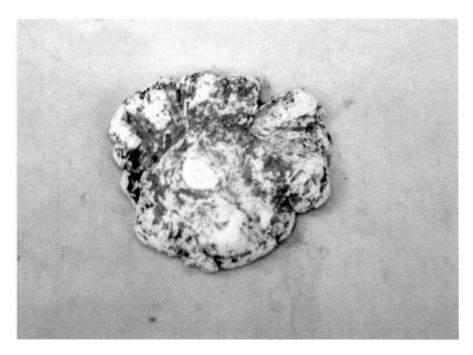

This exploded bullet from a raider's revolver is part of the "Souvenirs of the St. Albans Raid, October 19, 1864" box at the Vermont Historical Society. The historical items, documents and photographs in the collection originally belonged to John Branch Sr., who donated a custom-made storage box to the society before St. Albans had its own historical society. This oxidized bullet ball was attached to a letter that reads: "This ball was fired at Mr. Conger, who stood on the steps leading into the saloon under Smith's clothing store in St. Albans, by the Rebel Raiders who robbed the banks and attempted to burn the village—the ball struck the corner of the store and was picked up by me. H.E. Tucker." *Courtesy of the Vermont Historical Society. Photo by Michelle Arnosky Sherburne.*

and Maiden Lane. There, he found Elinus Morrison, a prominent New Hampshire building contractor in charge of the Welden project, and alerted him of the invasion. Morrison gathered several men and ran toward the scene to help. The men ran through the alley near Miss Beattie's Millinery Shop with Fuller in the lead.

When Young saw Fuller, he fired. But Fuller dodged behind one of the elm trees. Morrison, trying to escape the gunfire, intended to run into the millinery shop but was shot through the hand, and the bullet went into his abdomen.

Seventeen-year-old seamstress Adaliza Blakely was on her break in the millinery shop when she heard commotion and gunshots outside. She

A view of Miss Beattie's Millinery Shop on North Main Street, where Elinus Morrison was shot on the sidewalk by Lieutenant Bennett Young. Erasmus Fuller was able to use the elm trees in front of the stores as cover from the gunfire, but Morrison wasn't so fortunate. Fuller ran through the alley behind the elm tree on the far right to reach the Welden House construction and alert Morrison and his workers of the raid. *Courtesy of the St. Albans Historical Society and Museum.*

The sixth illustration in the November 12, 1864 edition of *Frank Leslie's Illustrated Newspaper*, titled "The Murder of Mr. E.J. Morrison." Elinus Morrison became the only casualty of the St. Albans Raid when he was shot by Lieutenant Young as he tried to retreat into Miss Beattie's Millinery Shop on Main Street. *Courtesy of Michelle Arnosky Sherburne.*

saw Young holding two pistols and standing beside his horse, about ten or twelve feet away from Morrison and the front of the shop. Blakely recognized Young as a man she had seen hanging around the Tremont Hotel earlier. She later testified at the Morrison inquest, "I saw this man with the pistols, above mentioned, fire twice with his pistols before Mr. Morrison was wounded."

Joined by other raiders, Young mounted his horse and moved on as Morrison lay wounded. Fuller and Marcus Wilson, who had witnessed the shooting, carried Morrison to L.L. Dutcher's drugstore down the street. Dr. Seth Day went to the drugstore and examined Morrison. At Morrison's inquest, Fuller testified, "I saw a wound a little above and anterior to the left hip bone and apparently penetrating the abdomen."

After the bank robberies, Young ordered his men to torch the American House and stores on Main Street. But the Greek fire didn't have the destructive effect they had hoped for. When it hit the building walls, it made a minor explosion but fizzled out because the buildings were so wet. No damage was done.

Gunshots, screaming, shouts and minor explosions alerted those indoors that something was happening on Main Street. Photographer Leonard Cross was in his studio on Main Street and went to the doorway to see what all the ruckus was about. "What are you trying to celebrate here?" Cross asked. A raider passing by shot at Cross but missed, the bullet lodging in the doorframe.

It was nearing the end of the school day at St. Albans Academy. Principal Dorsey Taylor was conducting an assembly on the third floor when he was given a disturbing message about the town being invaded by bank robbers. Trying to remain calm and composed, Taylor announced, "Little dears, wicked men have done very bad things here. Now do as you are told. Go down the stairs quietly to your rooms."

Opposite, top: Dutcher's drugstore, where the wounded Elinus Morrison was carried during the St. Albans Raid. In this photo, L.L. Dutcher is wearing a top hat in the front of the wagon while the boy, Alfred L. Dutcher, is riding on top of the load in the back. *Courtesy of the St. Albans Historical Society and Museum.*

Opposite, bottom: The exterior of the St. Albans Historical Museum on Church Street. During the St. Albans Raid, this building housed the St. Albans Academy. The school's principal and teachers kept the children safe while the raid was going on. *Photo by Michelle Arnosky Sherburne.*

Teacher Cora Burgess Wood later wrote, "I was sitting with my children near a window and I saw men running on Lake Street toward Main carrying iron bars, which we learned afterward were taken from the foundry. I also noticed an unusual commotion on the park…it is still a mystery how those frightened children descended the stairs safely and were gathered into their rooms."

As they filed out of the third-floor hall to the stairwell, students peered out the windows and could see commotion on the Village Green. Burgess wrote, "When the doors were closed my children were hopeless and panic stricken. They wanted to go home. They were going to be killed—burned up. Pandemonium reigned supreme for an hour or more—when the doors were opened and they were released running home to their mothers."

Captain George Conger, a recently returned veteran, testified at the raiders' trial:

> *I saw a great crowd of people towards the south part of the business portion of the village, around the American House and one of the banks. I met one Basford running his horse towards me, and he said, "What is going on down the street? There are men with pistols, taking horses from the stables." [He] wanted to know what it all meant. I said to him, "It is a regular raid." I then jumped from my team and came south. The first one of the band I met was in command, whom I afterwards learned was Lieutenant Bennett H. Young, as he gave me his name and that of his orderly. He said, "Are you a soldier?" I said, "No." Then he said, "You are my prisoner. Come with me to the other side of the green, opposite the American House."*

Young left a raider to take Conger across the street. Conger saw a number of people held hostage and decided to break away from his captor. He ran to the American House and then went downstairs and out the back door onto Lake Street. He spread the alarm that the town was being raided. Conger rallied people to arm themselves, shouting, "Bring on your arms for a fight; there is a regular raid on St. Albans."

The raiders had congregated in front of Brainerd's Store down beyond Tremont Hotel on Main Street, and the controlled atmosphere had begun to turn to chaos as more townspeople learned of the goings-on. In his book *The St. Albans Raid: 19 October 1864*, Carl Johnson wrote, "The Raiders were finding the streets rapidly filling with angry citizens, more of whom were coming with firearms. The Raiders knew that they were beginning to lose

A view of North Main Street in St. Albans with the American House on the left and the Franklin County Bank beside it. Note the muddy street on the right side near the Village Green where the St. Albans raiders held citizens hostage. At the time of the raid, there was the wooden sidewalk, fence and drainage ditch, as seen here. *Courtesy of St. Albans Historical Society and Museum.*

their 'control' of the town. Bennett Young was heard to repeat several times, 'Keep cool boys, keep cool.'"

Conger and a number of townspeople marched down Main Street in pursuit of the raiders, firing shots all the while.

When Young decided it was time to leave, he shouted, "Are we met?" And the raiders shouted, "We are met!" The raiders galloped north out of town, firing shots and shouting their "Rebel yells." As they fled, St. Albans resident Wilder Gilson, armed with his rifle, fired at them and hit raider Charles Higbee in the left shoulder. The bullet crossed Higbee's chest and traveled through his right shoulder.

The telegraph operator down at the rail yard sent the following message to Governor John Smith in Montpelier: "Southern raiders are in town, robbing banks, shooting citizens and burning houses." (One of Young's oversights was that he didn't think about the telegraph office down at the railroad station. Wires could have been cut to prevent spreading the news of the raid any farther than city limits.)

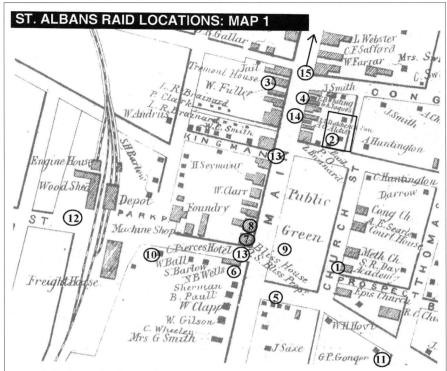

ST. ALBANS RAID LOCATIONS: MAP 1

1. St. Albans Academy, where students and teachers witnessed the Raid
2. Construction location of Welden House in 1864
3. Tremont Hotel, Bennett Young and others stayed there. Young sounds signal out front of Tremont to start Raid
4. Elinus Morrison shot in front of Miss Beattie's Shop by Bennett Young
5. First National Bank robbed
6. St. Albans Bank robbed
7. American House (formerly Bliss House), Raiders stayed here
8. Franklin County Bank robbed
9. Location on Public Green where townspeople were held hostage by Raiders
10. St. Albans House, Raiders stayed here
11. Capt. George Conger's house where he left and came upon the Raiders' on Main Street corraling residents to Green
12. Railyard included Freight House, Machine Shop, Depot, Telegraph Office, Engine House and Wood Shop, where over 400 workers were working unaware of the Raid events.
13. Guard posted to keep Raid area secure.
14. L.L. Dutcher's Drug Store where injured Morrison was taken.
15. Direction Raiders escaped out of town

This map, based on an 1857 Walling map of Franklin County and St. Albans Village, shows the locations of raid events. *Walling map courtesy of www.old-maps.com. Graphic design by Michelle Arnosky Sherburne.*

The raid lasted only half an hour, but this terrorist attack felt much longer. J.B. Baldwin, train conductor of the Rouses Point–Troy (NY) line, witnessed the raid while on vacation in St. Albans, and it was reported in the *Troy Times* on October 20.

Baldwin stated that he could "scarcely realize that it all happened, and that so much was done in so short a time. The guerrillas having all secured horses and saddles, commenced their retreat. They abandoned the prisoners and rode off northward, firing their pistols as they proceeded."

Chapter 11

THE ESCAPE

Lieutenant Young and the raiders rode north out of town and instead of heading to Swanton as planned, veered off onto Plank Road toward Sheldon. It has been reported that they made a quick stop at a house four or five miles up Plank Road because Young knew that the Raider Higbee was shot and would not travel well.

It was reported in Carl Johnson's book that Young left the wounded Higbee in the care of a woman and paid her well. She was to take him to Canada when he was able. Young remained at the house to settle things about Higbee and sent the rest of the raiders on their way.

Authors Daniel Rush and E. Gale Pewitt wrote the following, based on information obtained during a 1908 interview of Colonel Bennett Young by George Anderson, in a publication titled *The St. Albans Raiders*: "It is still a mystery how Young found and successfully bribed this unnamed woman during their frantic flight, but he apparently stayed behind to seal the deal and somehow managed to elude the posse through the night as he tried to rejoin his men…Higbee was smuggled into Montreal in a hay wagon a few days later and, despite rumors to the contrary, eventually recovered from his wounds." This would explain why Young had separated from his men and traveled north through Berkshire alone.

As for the rest of the raiders, it was well after 3:30 p.m. by the time they reached the end of Plank Road. They continued on East Sheldon Road headed to Sheldon. Lieutenant Colonel Reuben Benton wrote of the conditions in his "Personal Recollections": "At that time all the roads in the valleys of the streams and on ground near Lake Champlain were almost impassable. There had been a long succession of rainy weather, and the streams were all full and the wet parts of the road very muddy." This might have been why the raiders chose not to follow the route from St. Albans to Swanton along the lake. They stayed on the high ground and traveled the hills north to Sheldon.

But even then, after all the recent rain, all roads going into and out of St. Albans were muddy. In addition, the raiders had stolen horses that were not meant for long-term or fast riding—they definitely were not the cavalry horses to which they were accustomed. The raiders knew they had to cover a significant distance, so they would have had the horses do a slow trot. It was slow traveling in the mud—the raiders might have traveled no more than seven miles per hour.

Near the Sheldon-Fairfield town line, the raiders came upon a farmer on horseback. Vermont nineteenth-century historian Abigail Hemenway recounts the story in her "Raid of '64," published in the *Vermont Historical Gazetteer*:

> *A laughable incident occurred on the way to Sheldon. Just this side of the village, in the woods, they met a farmer on a good substantial horse, which one of them wanted in exchange for the one he was riding…Without words or ceremony, they drew the astonished farmer from his horse, which one of them quickly mounted, leaving his own jaded, panting animal in its place, when they dashed off rapidly as before. In mute and puzzled amazement, the farmer remained standing in the road, until the St. Albans party, riding like the others at full speed, came in sight. He, supposing them to be another portion of the body of whom he had been robbed, ran for life across the field, and the St. Albans party, recognizing the horse mistaking him for one of the robbers, gave chase, firing repeatedly at him, and gave it up only when their further progress was checked by swampy ground.*

The farmer remained in the woods until he deemed it safe to come out.

The raiders made it to Sheldon, where they found a hay wagon near the Sheldon Covered Bridge over Black Creek. They rode through the bridge, and then one raider moved the wagon onto the bridge, followed by another raider who threw a bottle of Greek fire on the hay. But once again, as the raiders rode off, the Greek fire only smoldered. Locals were able to extinguish it before it burned the wagon or the bridge.

Half a mile north, the raiders reached the Missisquoi Bank across from Colonel Alfred Keith's house. They all stopped, dismounted and realized it was too late to rob this bank because it had already closed. The raiders didn't

This illustration of the Sheldon Covered Bridge being set afire by retreating St. Albans raiders was the third appearing in the November 12, 1864 edition of *Frank Leslie's Illustrated Newspaper. Courtesy of Michelle Arnosky Sherburne.*

The Sheldon Covered Bridge crossed over the Black Creek in the middle of Sheldon. The raiders tried to set fire to the bridge to slow down the pursuing posse. *Courtesy of St. Albans Historical Society and Museum. Photo by Michelle Arnosky Sherburne.*

have any equipment to break down doors, any dynamite to blast their way into vaults or any wagons or places to transport more than they could carry. They also didn't have time.

The raiders milled around on the road. It was about 4:30 p.m.

Meanwhile, inside the bank, Homer G. Hubbell and other Missisquoi Bank employees saw the group of men outside and probably hid, not knowing what they were up to. They would not have been aware of the St. Albans event, but the sight of twenty-plus men on horseback all carrying revolvers must have alerted them that danger was afoot. Hubbell later reported, "I can assure you that such a band of followers are quite formidable in appearances. We had the pleasure of seeing every one of them. They carried Colts, Navy or Cavalry revolvers, and had 3 each on average." He wrote from Sheldon to his father on October 21 and stated that, at the bank, "We are O.K. & today I sent to Boston all our funds so that we have nothing to lose."

Across the valley near the cemetery, the first St. Albans posse led by Captain George Conger had reached this point and would have been able to see the raiders off in the distance. It might have appeared that another bank robbery was in progress.

It is not known whether Colonel Keith was home at the time raiders were in his yard that day. Carl Johnson wrote that Keith was the president of the Missisquoi Bank and had served in the Sixth Vermont Regiment. Later, he would become the commanding officer of the sixty volunteer soldiers for the Sheldon Provisional Militia and the acting assistant adjutant general in St. Albans, all in response to the raid.

Instead of robbing Keith's bank, they only stole a horse from his barn, which they then tried to burn. Once again, the ineffective incendiary material failed to work as the raiders took off.

After that stop, there is some question whether the Raiders split up. A mile north of Sheldon, they could have done this with a party heading on Kane Road through Franklin northward to the Canadian border. John Branch, raid eyewitness and historian, believed that was the case.

It is unclear what route Lieutenant Young took, but he might have left Plank Road and headed to Berkshire Center. According to Rush and Pewitt in *The St. Albans Raiders*, it was reported that he stopped at the E.S. Stevens farmhouse in Berkshire and paid the man's son to sneak him across the Canadian border.

By this time, it was around 6:00 p.m. and getting dark. The rest of the raiders continued on the East Sheldon Road to Enosburg Falls, crossing the Missisquoi River through another covered bridge. It was reported they might have tried to burn that bridge as well. As they rode toward West Berkshire,

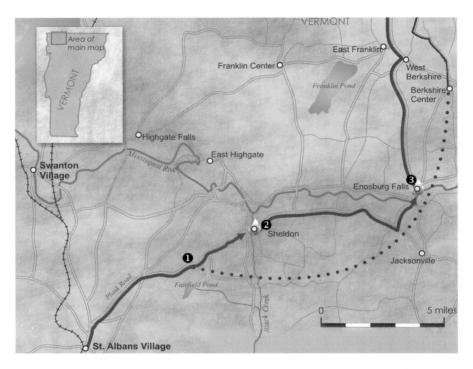

This map shows the routes taken by the St. Albans raiders to escape to Canada. The main route, marked by a solid line with arrows, began on Plank Road and continued through Sheldon, Enosburg Falls and north to West Berkshire and East Franklin before crossing over the Canadian border. The dotted line represents the possible route that Lieutenant Young took alone north to Canada. Number 1 denotes the possible location of the house where wounded raider Charles Higbee was left to be cared for, as per Young's orders. Numbers 2 and 3 denote covered bridges in Sheldon and Enosburg Falls that the raiders crossed and attempted to burn to slow the posse. "Escape Routes to Canada of the St. Albans Raiders—Oct. 19–20, 1864," published in *The St. Albans Raiders*, by Daniel S. Rush and E. Gale Pewitt. *Map illustrations by Dudley Pewitt Swiney and Kristin Risinger.*

it was reported that some raiders stopped at the Phoenix Hotel (which is still standing) for a brief break.

After a day's journey and traveling about twenty-five miles, the raiders crossed into Canada around 8:00 p.m. Another division occurred, with some riding off to Frelighsburg and others going farther north to Stanbridge East, Quebec. The raiders were sure that the Vermonters would not pursue them into Canada, so they were ready to collapse. The orders were to find a place and get some sleep. The plan was to meet again in Montreal.

THE POSSES

As the raiders galloped out of town, Captain George Conger had already organized a posse of about fifty men, who took pursuit on horseback or in carriages, wagons or buggies. They grabbed whatever they could find, anything from pitchforks to shotguns, to defend themselves. Conger's posse headed toward Sheldon.

A second posse was organized by Governor Smith's brother-in-law, Farrand Stewart Stranahan, and John Newton, former soldiers from the 1856 St. Albans militia called the Ransom Guard and Civil War veterans.

Their posse consisted of forty men, and they headed toward Franklin.

Carl Johnson wrote that county sheriff Renesselear Sherman, who had been in Burlington all day, returned to town as the posses were being organized. He learned that his fifteen-year-old son, Frederick, was with one of the posses preparing to leave. Sherman took Frederick and locked him in a jail cell and joined the posse himself.

Captain George P. Conger led the first St. Albans posse, about fifty men, in pursuit of the raiders on October 19, 1864. Captain Conger had served in the First Vermont Cavalry Regiment, Company B. *Courtesy of St. Albans Historical Society and Museum.*

Other St. Albanians who were part of the posses were Wilder Gilson, Erasmus Fuller, Leonard Cross, Charles A. Marvin, George Beals, William Farrar and Conger's nineteen-year-old son, George Steven Conger. *St. Albans Messenger* reporter William Whiting started out with the posse but was thrown from his horse and had to return to town.

Conger's posse followed fresh hoofprints on the muddy roads, and it was reported that bank notes were seen scattered along the roadsides. Conger's posse was on the trail and crossed the Canadian border. But Captain Conger decided that the posse was beyond its jurisdiction in Canada, so he contacted George Wells, the bailiff in Frelighsburg, and informed him of the robberies and raiders. Then, Conger's posse returned to Vermont.

With the two posses tracking the raiders, the alarm had been sounded and Governor Smith alerted. He set into motion state militia and sent messages to Burlington and to Washington.

From the War Department headquarters in New York City, General John Dix issued an order via telegraph to Conger: "Put a discreet officer in command and, if the raiders can't be found on this side of the line, pursue them into Canada if necessary and destroy them." Conger didn't receive Dix's order until the morning of October 20. Upon learning of Dix's order, President Lincoln immediately rescinded it to save violating Canadian neutrality laws and causing an international incident.

Dix had been overzealous and then had to backpedal. So on October 20, 1864, from the Department of the East headquarters in New York City, Dix sent the following message to Provost Marshal Redfield Proctor in Burlington: "What news from Saint Albans? I trust the officer understood my order in regard to pursuing the rebel raiders into Canada. It is only in case they are found on our side of the line, and the pursuit then must be instant and continuous. Advise him so."

The Stranahan-Newton posse did cross into Canada; however, it did not retreat.

Chapter 12

VERMONT'S CALL TO ARMS AFTER THE RAID

No time was wasted before Governor Smith ordered immediate protection of the state.

In less than twenty-four hours, Vermont's railroads, bridges, water routes on Lake Champlain and roads were guarded by the fastest recruited militia during the Civil War.

Caught by surprise at St. Albans, Vermonters were not going to stand for any more raids. The tenacity and ingenuity of Vermonters was exemplified in their immediate response to protect their state. Just as Vermonters didn't hesitate to answer Lincoln's call to arms when the Civil War began in April 1861, they answered immediately. The war had come to the Green Mountain state.

The first response Governor Smith had was to stop the trains in the state. He was not aware of how the raiders were escaping, and being president of the railroad, he could do that immediately. From the Executive Chamber on October 19, Smith gave the following order: "Col. R.C. Benton is hereby authorized to take charge of the trains on the Vt. Central R.R. Conductors, Engineers and other officials will obey his orders."

The governor then ordered Adjutant General Peter T. Washburn to issue a number of executive orders to Lieutenant Colonel Reuben Benton in St. Albans and Colonel Redfield Proctor in Burlington to form a state militia. Some of Washburn's first orders were:

Governor John Gregory Smith was the twenty-eighth governor of Vermont, serving from 1863 to 1865. He protected the state during the St. Albans Raid and issued a state militia force to safeguard the town from any future raids. *Courtesy of the University of Vermont Libraries, Special Collections, Bailey/Howe Library.*

State of Vermont,
Executive Chamber, St. Albans, Oct. 19, 1864.

Lieut. Col. R.C. Benton will at once proceed to Burlington and thence, with such arms and ammunition as are necessary, will proceed to repel rebel raid now in progress. He is authorized to organize such force as may be necessary north of Burlington, and will take command of all forces north of that point, reporting to Col. Redfield Proctor, at Burlington, from time to time.

By order of the Governor,
PETER T. WASHBURN,
Adjt. & Ins. General.

Montpelier, Vt., Oct. 19, 1864.
Col. Redfield Proctor, Burlington, Vt.

Organize and arm two companies of one hundred men each in Burlington to-night. Send two hundred muskets with equipments and eight thousand rounds of ammunition to this place first train; keep eight hundred in Burlington, and send one thousand to Col. Benton.

P.T. WASHBURN,
Adjt. & Ins. Gen.

Deliver immediately.

Colonel Proctor was immediately sent to Burlington with directions to provide for the defense of that place and to take command of all forces in the northwestern part of the state. Lieutenant Colonel Benton was dispatched to St. Albans, and he organized defense forces in Franklin County. Lieutenant Colonel William W. Grout, of Barton, was ordered by telegram to organize and arm such force to protect the banks at Derby Line and Irasburgh.

Benton shared in his "Personal Recollections" that the governor "gave me unlimited control of the railroad and all its appliances, and commanding every officer and employee of the road to obey my orders." Following the governor's directives, Benton went to Montpelier first to organize a military company there and then was sent to St. Albans to take "immediate measures to repel the invaders and to prevent the recurrence of similar raids."

Upon arriving in St. Albans, Benton wrote, "I found the streets pretty well lined with crowds of people very much excited as one would naturally expect, but in the darkness (for there were scarcely any street lamps) it was impossible to discover whether they were friends or foes that composed the crowd."

Detachments from the Veteran Reserve Corps were sent to St. Albans the night of October 19 from Brattleboro, Montpelier and Burlington. Arriving the night of the raid, arms and ammunition were sent from the arsenal at Vergennes and distributed to soldiers in Burlington, St. Albans and Montpelier.

Secretary of War Edwin Stanton had arms and ammunition shipped from the Vergennes arsenal to St. Albans. Over the next few days, five hundreds stands of arms including carbines, pistols, sabers and cavalry equipment were shipped. Two six-pound 1840 solid brass cannon were shipped to town and placed at the north end of Main Street. On the night of October 19,

ORLEANS COUNTY
AWAKE
REBELS IN VERMONT!

St. Johnsbury, Oct. 19, 1864.
By Telegraph from Montpelier to Col. Grout:

Lieut. Col. Wm. W. Grout will immediately proceed to take such measures as may be necessary to organize and arm such force as may be necessary to protect the Banks of Irasburgh and Derby Line, from a

REBEL RAID NOW BEING MADE IN VERMONT!

and is hereby authorised to take command of all forces which he may raise. He will report to this office as often as possible.   By order of the Governor,

P.T. WASHBURN,

Adjutant and Inspector General.

The above telegram was received by me

at 12 o'clock last night, and the special messenger who brought it from St. Johnsbury, also brought the rumor that a rebel raiding party from Canada had

Entered St. Albans,

and murdered her citizens, and in obedience to the above order I call upon every man who has a musket or rifle to

REPORT AT ONCE

for military duty during the emergency.   Bring powder and ball. Those in Irasburgh and vicinity will report at Irasburgh to Rev. J. H. Woodward, whose orders they will obey. Those in Derby and vicinity will report at Derby Line to Col. B.H. Steele, whose orders they will obey. Those in Barton and vicinity will report at Barton to Capt. George H. Blake, whose orders they will obey. Those in Newport and vicinity will report at Newport to Capt. L. H. Bisbee, whose orders they will obey. Those in Troy and vicinity will report at North Troy to Hon. A.J. Rowell, whose orders they will obey.

BARTON, OCTOBER 20, 1864.

WM. W. GROUT,
Commanding Provisional Forces.

A rendition of a poster warning Vermont residents of the "Rebels in Vermont!" and the possibility of additional Confederate raids. *Graphic design by Michelle Arnosky Sherburne.*

volunteer companies were organized at presumed target locations such as St. Albans, Burlington, Newport and Montpelier and, the next morning, reported for duty. In all, there were approximately 1,300 men in place to defend Vermont.

Upon word of the St. Albans Raid, panic ensued in Burlington. There were reports that one of the Champlain Transportation Company steamers had been hijacked. The company president issued orders to Rouses Point to move the steamer moorings farther out into the lake for protection. He armed the steamer crews with revolvers, and traffic at Rouses Point was guarded.

In Burlington, residents gathered in large groups, and men volunteered for a military unit that was dispatched to St. Albans. Over the next few months, sales of weapons increased drastically, and it was hard for store owners to keep them in demand.

Brattleboro sent over 130 soldiers to St. Albans upon notification of the state of emergency. Major William Austine in Brattleboro stated that he "received the inclosed [sic] telegram at 7 p.m. on the 19th instant. At once I collected about 100 convalescents and 30 of the Veteran Reserve Corps, with two officers, from the general hospital here, and left at 9 p.m. (the earliest train to be had), arriving at Saint Albans (the place of residence of the Governor), a distance of 200 miles, at 8 o'clock the next morning." Austine, serving as the acting assistant provost marshal and military commander, reported to the headquarters of the Department of the East in New York City on October 23.

Offers of assistance were sent from various Vermont towns that were ready and willing to travel to St. Albans to help fight off more raiders. Instead, the governor issued militia guards.

Since Newport was assumed to be a possible target for an expected second raid, Governor Smith ordered the Norwich cadets to take an express train there on the day of the raid. Reverend Howard F. Hill, one of the cadets sent to Newport, wrote about his observations in "The History of Norwich University: The St. Albans Raid," published in *The Vermonter* magazine in September 1899. Hill wrote:

> *On arrival, we found Newport in wild excitement…The Newport people had organized a company most fearfully and wonderfully armed…We were met by this array at the depot. There was good, untutored stuff in these bodies. On alighting from the cars, we were ordered to load our Springfields with ball cartridge, and marched to the wharf to receive an incoming steamer, then visible in the dusk, as the possible carrier of raiders. We formed with the Newporters as support. The first few minutes were big*

with possibilities, but nothing happened…While the outing thus recorded was neither bloody nor protracted, it is not romancing to say that the real war spirit was afire in us. All were ready for larger things, and, it is not to be doubted, would have met them creditably. We at least looked for a considerable term of serious service, but back to Norwich we went on Saturday, having, perhaps, "saved the country." At any rate, we had done something to uphold the honor of Vermont and cheer its anxious people.

By Saturday, October 21, the Newport militia had been established and was ready to protect the town and surrounding area, so the Norwich cadets were sent back to the university.

Oscar Burton, president of the Champlain Transportation Company on Lake Champlain, sent word to Rouses Point, New York, to ready crews with revolvers and to direct boats to be anchored away from the wharves to protect them from being captured by the raiders.

George Randall of Newbury, Vermont, was working at Rouses Point along with Edmund Chittenden. Years later, in a letter to Randall, Chittenden recalled that "there were about 14 men on the muster roll to guard Rouses Point as part of the Frontier Militia." He continued:

We were enrolled by order of the N.Y. Secy. of State and armed with guns such as from Albany N.Y. or…Arsenal. I don't remember which, but think the latter, we did six weeks service—don't know that anyone ever asked for or received any pay and do not remember that we were each mustered in or out—I do remember that we were inspected by one Capt. Smith of the Regular army & then in command at Ft. Montgomery and of the Invalid Corps there stationed at Wind Mill Point and along the Frontier.

On the other side of the border, a large militia troop was stationed for protection by the Canadian government as well.

Chapter 13

THE ARRESTS

In the early morning hours of Thursday, October 20, Lord Charles Monck received a message from Vermont governor Smith informing him of St. Albans Raid and that the perpetrators had escaped and crossed into Canada. Monck then contacted Judge Charles J. Coursol in Montreal to send a police force to capture the raiders. The Canadians also sent militia to the border in the event that another raiding party should enter Canada and to prevent more Americans from pursuing the raiders. St. Albans posse members Cross, Smith and Holmes remained in Stanbridge East and notified Justice of the Peace Henry Whitman of the raid and the necessity for cooperation.

Local Canadian authorities in Frelighsburg and Stanbridge East and a remnant of the St. Albans posse were able to locate and capture fourteen of the raiders. It was reported that all of the raiders' clothes were splattered with mud; it appeared they had simply collapsed after making it into Canada. They didn't think they would be pursued and were exhausted. Two hours later, George Wells, the bailiff in Frelighsburg, located Charles Swagar and Caleb Wallace in town, and the first arrests were made at 10:00 p.m.

About 1:00 a.m., Whitman's group found Thomas Collins at Henry Bacon's hotel and arrested him. Whitman testified at the first November trial that "the prisoner, Collins, came into Henry Bacon's hotel, in Stanbridge East, between twelve and one o'clock in that night. I was in the hotel at the time, and ordered him into custody, and placed keepers over him and the prisoner, Samuel Eugene Lackey, and was arrested on the side-walk near Mr. Bacon's hotel." Lackey and Collins had stolen money on them, and

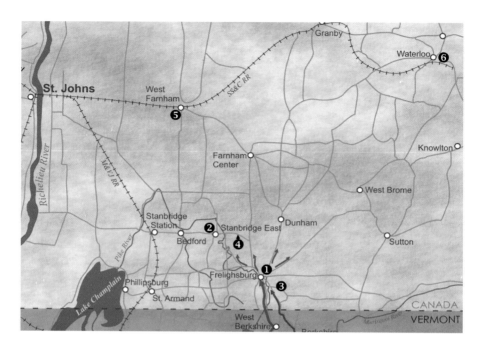

This map shows the locations where the raiders were captured. Number 1 is where Swagar and Wallace were captured on October 19 and Squire Tevis was captured on October 20; number 2 denotes where Bruce, Spurr, Collins and Lackey were captured on October 20; number 3 is where Lieutenant Young was captured by Erasmus Fuller and others on October 20; number 4 is where Doty and McGrorty were located in a barn on October 21; number 5 is the location where Scott was captured on October 20 and Gregg arrested at a railroad station on October 21; and number 6 is where Moore was captured on a train on October 21. "Capture Sites of 14 of the St. Albans Raiders—Oct. 19–24, 1864," published in *The St. Albans Raiders*, by Daniel S. Rush and E. Gale Pewitt. *Map illustrations by Dudley Pewitt Swiney and Kristin Risinger.*

Whitman stated in his testimony that "they were all dressed in common civilians' dress."

In Stanbridge East, two raiders were asleep in a room at Elder's Tavern. Whitman, local bailiff Edmund Knight and six other men, including St. Albans photographer Leonard Cross, arrived at the tavern around 3:00 a.m. and broke down the door, surprising Alamanda Bruce and Marcus Spurr. One of the posse members handcuffed the raiders and, searching under their pillows, found revolvers and loose packages of cash. Their coat pockets and trouser pockets also had packages of money and treasury notes in them. Whitman later testified, "Two of them, namely, Bruce and Spurr, were in bed at a tavern kept in the village of Stanbridge by one William Elder; and

Alamanda Bruce served in Company A of the Sixth Kentucky Cavalry. Bruce, twenty-three at the time of the raid, was captured and sent to Camp Douglas but later escaped. He was one of the escapees commissioned for the Camp Douglas attempt. *Courtesy of St. Albans Historical Society and Museum.*

I made prisoners of them, and put keepers over them." Whitman observed that the mens' clothes were spotted with mud and that some of them even had mud on their faces, "having the appearance of persons who had travelled rapidly over muddy roads."

Lieutenant Young had made it to Frelighsburg by Thursday morning as well. He had stopped at a farmhouse, where he was arrested by officials. With the Canadian officials were St. Albans posse members led by Erasmus Fuller and George Beals. Fuller was the first to enter the house, where he found Young in the kitchen. Fuller then jumped on Young, and the two men began to fight. Young was overcome and placed into a wagon by the officials. He wouldn't give up easily, however, and managed to knock the driver off the wagon and tried to drive away. He was caught again by Fuller's men.

Young protested the arrest by Americans on Canadian soil. It was a violation of Canadian neutrality laws, and the fact that the St. Albans posse wanted to return him to the States for prosecution would be a violation of British law. But bailiff George Wells and Canadian officers arrived in time to take over the arrest with proper jurisdiction.

Above: The final St. Alban's Raid illustration in the November 12, 1864 edition of *Frank Leslie's Illustrated Newspaper* depicts the arrest of two of the raiders and the recovery of some money at a hotel in Stanbridge East, Quebec, by members of the St. Albans posse and Canadian authorities. *Courtesy of Michelle Arnosky Sherburne.*

Left: Marcus Antonius Spurr, twenty at the time of the St. Albans Raid, served in Company A of the Eighth Kentucky Calvary and also was captured. He escaped Camp Douglas and later was one of the soldiers assigned to the failed Camp Douglas prisoner release attempt. *Courtesy of St. Albans Historical Society and Museum.*

Squire Turner Tevis, Company B, Seventh Kentucky Cavalry, was captured and sent to Camp Morton. After escaping, he served as one of the Camp Douglas attack soldiers and, later, as one of Young's Retributors. *Courtesy of St. Albans Historical Society and Museum.*

James Alexander Doty, Company A, Sixth Kentucky Calvary, was one of the prisoners who escaped from Camp Douglas. *Courtesy of St. Albans Historical Society and Museum.*

On the night of October 20, Squire Tevis was caught near a house at Frelighsburg and was arrested there. Rush and Pewitt's research reported that Tevis had buried money in the house's basement, in the barn and in a nearby cornfield. The total Tevis had buried was approximately $17,500.

George Scott was about to get on a train at the railroad station in Farnham when officials arrested him. Dudley Moore had stayed at Hall's Hotel in Waterlook but was arrested on the train at Waterloo. Samuel Gregg was also captured at the Waterloo station. The Whitman posse located James Doty and Joseph McGrorty the following night, October 21, sleeping in a barn in Dunham.

Over the next few days, authorities rounded up raiders, most of whom were armed and in possession of stolen money. The amounts varied and were in the form of Franklin County Bank notes, U.S. treasury notes, St. Albans bank bills, bonds, loose coins and U.S. greenbacks.

Five days after the raid, on October 24, William Hutchinson paid a farmer to take him to the St. Lawrence River. That night, Hutchinson took off on a skiff headed for Montreal. Pursued by Judge Coursol's officers, Hutchinson thought he was getting away, only to be caught by the chief of police on the other side.

An actual twenty-dollar Franklin County Bank note stolen by the St. Albans Raiders on October 19, 1864, is in the collection of the St. Albans Historical Museum. The late Robert Houghton of St. Albans purchased a number of these bank notes at an auction in the South. The money had been saved by the family of raider Marcus Spurr, who had kept some as souvenirs. Houghton donated the notes to the museum. *Courtesy of St. Albans Historical Society and Museum. Photo by Michelle Arnosky Sherburne.*

Approximately $88,000 was recovered from the captured raiders, who were held in Frelighsburg for three days. No arrangements were made to return them to Vermont for prosecution.

A group of St. Albans residents interviewed Lieutenant Young while he was in the Frelighsburg jail. Oscar Kinchen wrote:

> *They called his attention to the fact that many widows and orphans would suffer as a consequence of the money that had been looted from their banks. But Young replied that this was "all very nice talk when applied to the northern people, but it had no significance, with the Northern armies subjugating the South with fire, sword and musket." He went on to remind his visitors of the suffering that the people of the South had endured, including those of his own kindred, as the consequence of the depredations that were being carried out by Union troops who spared neither the civilian population nor their private property.*

As for the rest of the raiders, they were able to escape one way or another. William Tevis reportedly disguised himself as a woman and worked his way back into the States, traveling through the blockades and eventually returning to Richmond. It was said that he reported to President Davis and gave his portion of the raid to the CSA.

The raiders thought the legal difficulties would be taken care of by the Confederate commissioners, but it became clear that the situation wouldn't be

William Tevis, twenty-four at the time of the raid, was in Company B of the Eighth Kentucky Cavalry. After being wounded, he was left in Kentucky, captured and then paroled. He ended up in Canada and was commissioned to be part of the Camp Douglas attempt. Stories tell that he escaped capture by disguising himself as a woman and making his way south. After the war, he traveled to Switzerland. He received a pardon by Secretary of State William Seward in 1866. *Photo courtesy of Stone Armentrout. Published in* The St. Albans Raiders, *by Daniel S. Rush and E. Gale Pewitt.*

resolved immediately. On October 21, raider Caleb Wallace sent the following telegram to George Sanders: "We are captured. Do what you can for us." Though Wallace sent the message to Sanders, Henry Whitman, who had arrested Bruce and Spurr, later testified that those two men had requested Whitman send a message to Clement Clay, a Confederate agent in Montreal, to make him aware they had been captured and to send help.

The Confederate commissioners responded quickly. George Sanders responded to the call for help and arrived in St. Johns to make arrangements for legal defense and for the welfare of the raiders.

It was during his brief imprisonment in Frelighsburg that Young wrote a letter, dated October 21, to the *Montreal Evening Telegraph* as his first official statement after the raid. Young wrote:

> *Through the columns of your journal I wish to make some statements to the people of Canada, regarding the recent operations in Vermont. I went there for the purpose of burning the town and surrounding villages in retaliation for the recent outrages committed in the Shenandoah Valley, and elsewhere in the Confederate States. I am a commissioned officer of the Provisional Army of the Confederate States, and have violated no laws of Canada. I do not wish my name coupled with the epithets now applied without the knowledge on the part of the people of Canada, as to who we are and what*

caused our action. I wish, also, to make a few statements as to how myself and party were taken. I was seized on Canadian soil by American citizens with arms in their hands and violently searched. My pocket-book was taken from me, and I was started towards the United States. I reached out my hand and caught the reins of my horse, when three pistols were leveled at my head, with threats to shoot the d——d scoundrel dead, if he moved. Some Canadian citizens then spoke up and the Americans, seeing the bailiff, started with me toward him, two of them holding arms in their hands. These statements can be proved by Canadian citizens. The Americans came into this place and even beyond it, brandishing guns and threatening to kill some of us even after we were in the hands of the English authorities. Surely the people of Vermont must have forgotten that the people of Canada are not in the midst of war, and ruled by a man despotic in his actions and supreme in his infamy. I am not afraid to go before the courts of Canada, and when the affair is investigated, I am satisfied that the citizens of Vermont, and not my party, will be found to be the violators of Canadian and English law. Some one, I hope, will be sent to investigate this breach of neutrality, and award to those American citizens doing armed duty in Canada, the just merit of their transgressions.

Bennett H. Young
First Lieutenant Provisional Army
Confederate States of America

As Kinchen reported in *Daredevils of the Confederate Army,* Governor Smith contacted Secretary of State William Seward in Washington on October 21 to inform him that eight raiders had been captured. He relayed the facts that the raiders had admitted guilt, that they had telegraphed Sanders for help and that counsel was arranged for them. He added, "These marauders claim that they are commissioned officers and enlisted men of the Confederate army, detailed to carry war on our border in this style."

The prisoners originally rounded up and held at Frelighsburg were transferred to the St. Johns military garrison on October 22. Lord Monck appointed Coursol to conduct a full investigation into the Vermont raid, the flight of the alleged perpetrators and the conflicting claims of ownership of the funds.

It was reported that $83,000 had been stolen from the St. Albans Bank, $75,000 from Franklin County Bank and $55,000 from First National Bank.

Chapter 14

THE ONLY RAID CASUALTY

After Elinus Morrison was shot by Lieutenant Bennett Young on the day of the raid, he was moved from L.L. Dutcher's drugstore to the American Hotel. Morrison was cared for at the hotel, and his wife, Mary, arrived from New Hampshire. He died two days after the raid. His death was reported in newspapers all over the country. On October 24, 1864, Montpelier's *Walton's Morning Journal* reported, "Mr. E.J. Morrison, wounded by the rebels at St. Albans, has since died, and his remains taken to Manchester, N.H." On the same day, the *St. Albans Messenger* printed the following:

> *As we announced yesterday, Mr. Morrison died from the effects of his wound, in the morning, after receiving the most skillful medical treatment that could be procured. Impressive funeral services were held at the American Hotel last evening where the deceased has for a long time boarded, the Rev. J. Isham Bliss, pastor of St. Luke's Church, officiating. The assemblage of people was very large, and much feeling was manifested. Mr. Morrison's remains were taken to Manchester to be buried there.*

An autopsy and inquest was ordered by the St. Albans Board of Selectmen and the inquest conducted by Justice of the Peace Leonard Gilman. A board of surgeons and physicians, including Day and Dr. John Branch, who had examined Morrison prior to his death, conducted the autopsy. Witnesses Erasmus Fuller, Adaliza Blakely and Myron Wilson were interviewed and their statements taken.

The Morrison family monument in Valley Cemetery, Manchester, New Hampshire, where building contractor Elinus Morrison is buried. Morrison was tragically murdered by Lieutenant Bennett Young during the St. Albans Raid in 1864. He was shot on the day of the raid and died two days later. *Photo by Michelle Arnosky Sherburne.*

Within a day, the conclusive results were recorded by Gilman: "After a careful consideration of all the testimony I have the honor to report that it is my belief that the said Elinus J. Morrison received his death wound from a pistol shot fired by one of a gang of armed raiders in St. Albans Village on the 19th day of October, 1864, while the said E. J. Morrison was quietly standing or walking along the sidewalk and herewith return the same to the Franklin County Court." A funeral service was held at the American Hotel and officiated by the Reverend J. Isham Bliss of St. Luke's Episcopal Church, another St. Albans building Morrison had constructed. His remains were taken to Manchester, where services were held at his home. Morrison was then buried in the Valley Cemetery in Manchester.

Who was Elinus J. Morrison, and why was he in St. Albans?

Morrison was a building contractor from Manchester, New Hampshire, working on the Welden Hotel in October 1864. He was a brick mason and building contractor who traveled to Pennsylvania, New York, Boston and upstate Vermont for contracts. He was proficient in designing buildings, railroad bridges and tunnels. In Burlington, he constructed a railroad tunnel in 1862 that now bears his name.

In St. Albans, his craftsmanship remains today in two of the four buildings he built in town. On Church Street, Morrison built the St. Albans Museum building (formerly the schoolhouse) and, next door, the Episcopal Church, which is made of calico stone. Two other buildings of Morrison's were the original First Congregational Church, which burned in the late 1800s, and the Welden Hotel, which also burned to the ground. In 1864, Morrison had returned to St. Albans, hired to build the five-story, two-hundred-room Welden Hotel.

In the *History of the Morison or Morrison Family*, Elinus was described as "medium height, rather thick-set, florid complexion, sandy hair and a stirring enterprising capable businessman." He was born and raised in Fairlee, Vermont. His parents, James and Martha Morrison, were farmers and had lived in Orford, New Hampshire, before moving across the Connecticut River to Fairlee. Elinus was the fifth of ten children. He had followed his older brother George to Manchester when he was a young man. George became a prominent lawyer there, and Elinus became successful in his building trade.

Elinus married Boscawen, New Hampshire native Mary Elliott in 1840, and the couple had six children over a sixteen-year period: Anna, Maria, Frank, Mary, George and Nellie. Elinus was fifty-two when he was murdered.

It was reported by Edward Sowles in his 1876 address to the Vermont Historical Society that Morrison was a Confederate sympathizer. According to Sowles, Morrison had apparently had conversations with some of the raiders at the American Hotel, where he was staying as well. Sowles reported that Morrison had disclosed to them his sentiments but did not realize the men were part of a planned future raid on the town. Of his untimely death, the family genealogy history stated that "he was killed by rebels at St. Albans" and "it seemed a strange providence that he should have fallen by an act of war while engaged in peaceable pursuits, hundreds of miles from any known hostile force."

It was tragic that a man such as Morrison, who had created beautiful buildings in St. Albans, would die simply because he had been at the wrong place at the wrong time.

Chapter 15

THE NEWS HITS THE PAPERS

Telegraph offices were buzzing and the printing presses at top speed on October 20, 1864. The event in a small northern Vermont town was ranked as important as the Union victory at Cedar Creek the same day. By the Friday after the raid, newspapers hit the streets with headlines such as "Alarm at Home!" and "Rebel Raid into St. Albans!" Newspapers all over the state informed Vermonters of the event. Hot off the presses all over the United States were similar headlines. On October 21, the *Vermont Watchman and State Journal* reported:

> *Startling Intelligence! Rebel Raid into St. Albans! BANKS ROBBED! A CITIZEN MURDERED! Dispatch to Governor Smith! The Legislature hastily Assembled. Prompt Measures for Defence. The following dispatches were received at about four o'clock this afternoon: Montpelier, Oct. 19, By Telegraph from St. Albans to B. Barlow: "There has been a rebel raid to this place and have robbed all the banks and have shot one or more men." J.D. Sowles. St. Albans, Oct. 19. To Gov. Smith: "There is a party of rebels here shouting and killing citizens. Have stolen as many as fifteen horses, and robbed all the banks. E.A. Smith." Gov. Smith hastily summoned the Legislature to assemble and communicated to them the above dispatches also the further intelligence that the soldiers of the invalid corps at Montpelier and Burlington about two hundred in number had been ordered forward. He had also directed the citizens of Burlington to organize for defence.*

That same day, the *Vermont Phoenix*, out of Brattleboro, reported:

> *Alarm at Home. The people of this Village were thrown into a state of excitement on Wednesday p.m. by a telegram from Montpelier stating that there was a raid upon St. Albans, that the raiders had robed* [sic] *the banks, and wounded several citizens. The bells were rung, the people collected, and in a short space of time about 100 men volunteered their services to go to the scene of action on the first train.*

The *Newport News* printed the story six days later:

> *On Thursday morning last, the good people of this village and vicinity were startled by a summons emanating from the adjutant-general of the State, calling upon the arms-bearing citizens to report immediately for duty; that the State had been invaded by land pirates from the neighboring provinces; that the village of St. Albans had been sacked, citizens murdered in cold blood, banks robbed of an immense amount of treasure, and all the crimes of the highwayman, the robber, and the incendiary committed within the borders of our gallant State, and within a Sabbath-day's journey of our quiet and flourishing village.*

In the Northeast Kingdom of Vermont, the October 29 *Danville North Star* reprinted a *Burlington Times* article that had run after the raid:

> *The citizens of St. Albans at first were completely astounded and paralyzed and hardly knew what to do, but the vigorous exertions and appeals of Capt. George P. Conger and Capt. J.W. Newton soon rallied a mounted force of some fifty picked men, who forthwith pursued the rebels, who had left town in the direction of Sheldon, robbing the farmers as they went along of saddles and bridles. The whole affair did not occupy over twenty minutes, and had even a small portion of the citizens on the ground had been decently armed, the marauders would have stood a small chance of escaping unharmed. Only one of them was wounded, and he slightly in the hand. He was wounded by a shot from Mr. Stephen Conger, son of Capt. Conger.*

Across the Canadian border, Montreal was issued reports about the raid, and by October 20, raiders had been arrested on Canadian soil. An article titled "Outrage of St. Albans" was from a special telegram received from the *Montreal Gazette* correspondent on the Vermont and Boston lines:

From October 1864 to April 1865, newspapers all over the North featured headlines about the St. Albans Raid and the subsequent arrests, trials and releases. *Courtesy of www. newspapers.com. Graphic design by Michelle Arnosky Sherburne.*

A party of 20 rebel raiders entered this place this p.m. shooting and killing the citizens. They robbed all the banks, stole 15 or 20 horses, killed 4 or 5 and wounded several. They have left town but are expected back soon with a large force. If there is no error or exaggeration in this statement, a gross outrage has been committed, in a peaceful and thriving village, situated on the Vermont Central Railway, a short distance from Rouses Point, and not far from the borders of Canada. It is not stated that the "raiders" took their departure from Canada, or whether they had gathered and concealed themselves near the village in which they committed their outrage. But there is enough to call for vigilance on the part of the Canadian Government. Probably many of our readers saw in the midnight despatches [sic] in our last impression that a Richmond paper (the Whig) threatened reprisal for the horrible destruction which has taken place in the Shenandoah Valley, by burning Northern towns; and that Canada was to be made one of the places of rendezvous.

News traveled quickly, and St. Albans was soon in headlines all across the North, including papers in Ohio, Kansas, Illinois, Wisconsin, Pennsylvania, New York and Massachusetts. From October 20, 1864, into June 1865, St. Albans Raid articles were appearing in newspapers in Canada and in Europe. Days after the raid, the telegraph offices were sending news all over the Canadian provinces, and newspapers there, like the *Colonial Standard* in Pictou, Nova Scotia, were running articles about the raid.

As far west as Wisconsin, in the Friday, October 21 morning edition of the *Daily Milwaukee News*, the headlines were about the Vermont attack:

Robbers Arrested. Burlington, VT., Oct. 20: Eight of the raiders who entered St. Albans and robbed the banks and murdered citizens have been caught and $50,000 of the money recovered. They were caught at Walbridge and Farnham, Canada East. The remainder have been seen on the road, and will probably also be arrested…St. Albans, Vt., Oct. 20.—Later advices from the parties who are pursuing the raiders, confirm the news of the capture of 8 of the freebooters and $50,000 of the stolen bank bills. Considerable excitement still prevails, though all apprehensions of any further danger at present from the marauders are entirely removed.

Four days after the raid, *Frank Leslie's Illustrated Newspaper* sent artist W.T. Crane and a reporter to research and collect visual images of the town. Crane worked with St. Albans photographer T.G. Richardson, who actually was an eyewitness to the raid. Richardson was one of about twelve townspeople who were held hostage on the Green. Crane worked from photographs of St. Albans streets to create eleven illustrations.

The November 12, 1864 edition of *Frank Leslie's Illustrated Newspaper* featured a two-page spread of raid illustrations that were made into woodcuts and printed like a storyboard of the raid. The following article was printed as well:

We devote a large space, this week, to illustrations of the recant rebel raid upon St. Alban's, Vermont. St. Albans is a flourishing town, situated three miles east of Lake Champlain, 23 miles from Rouse's Point—where the railroads converge, going North—and 10 miles from the Canada line. The raid was made upon it on the afternoon of Wednesday, the 19th Oct. Business hours had not passed and the banks were still open. The attacking party numbered 25 or 30 persons. These men had come over from Canada and quietly congregated at the various hotels in St. Albans, holding no noticeable communication and awakening no suspicion. Their plan was a bold one, and was successfully executed. On the day mentioned, at about three o'clock in the afternoon, they suddenly congregated, in squads, and made a simultaneous attack on the St. Albans, the Franklin County and the First National Banks. At each bank they drew their revolvers, threatening instant death to all the officers present if any resistance was made. They then robbed the drawers and vaults of all specie, bills and other valuable articles that they could lay their hands upon.

In the October 26, 1864 *New York Times*, it was reported that

the attack was well planned to take the town by surprise. Tuesday is the market day when the country people bring in their produce to sell, and when the streets are full of people. The next day, Wednesday, is uniformly the dullest day in the week, and but few persons are in town. At the time of the attack few people were in the streets. Few ladies were "shopping" and a few men were standing upon the sidewalks. The affair commenced shortly after 3 o'clock, and completed within half an hour, and the raiders had left the village. The traces of horses attached to wagons were cut, and where a collar was hard to come off over a horse's head, it was left on…In the course of their hasty retreat from St. Albans to the Canada line, they dropped bank bills and papers with which their

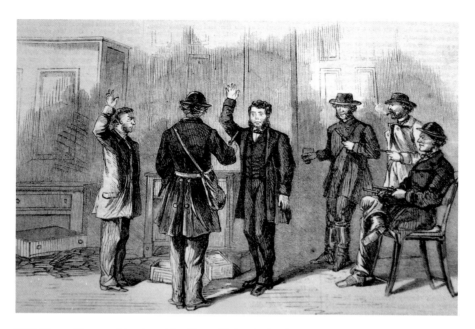

W.T. Crane illustrated bank cashier Cyrus Bishop being forced to take an oath of allegiance to the Confederate States of America during the raid on St. Albans Bank. This is the ninth image in the November 12, 1864 issue of *Frank Leslie's Illustrated Newspaper*. *Courtesy of Michelle Arnosky Sherburne.*

> *pockets were filled. Among them was a "high-falutin" address to the people of Vermont, in the style of Southern chivalry, threatening to burn all the villages and rob the banks.*

A reporter for the *Toronto Globe*, in a story that was reprinted in other newspapers such as the *New York Times*, wrote:

> *We are indebted to the kindness of the American Consul for the following additional particulars: "There were twenty-three persons concerned in this robbery, and the amount taken from the banks is $223,000, a portion of which, though the exact sum is unknown, has been found upon some of those arrested…In all probability it will be established that the St. Albans raiders were a gang of mere vulgar robbers, instigated to the outrage by the hope of booty alone, and they will at once be handed over to the United States authorities, to suffer the penalty of their daring crime.*

Bank employee Marcus Beardsley and St. Albans resident Jackson Clark are rescued from the Franklin County Bank vault in which the raiders had locked them. This is the fourth image in the November 12, 1864 issue of *Frank Leslie's Illustrated Newspaper*. *Courtesy of Michelle Arnosky Sherburne.*

On November 5, 1864, *Harper's Weekly* ran the following article:

> *In the afternoon of October 19 considerable disturbance was occasioned in St. Albans, Vermont, by the appearance in that town of several marauders from the Canada side who, under pretense of being Confederates, murdered a number of the citizens and stole a considerable sum of money from the banks. After accomplishing their object they returned into Canada. Captain Conger, with a detachment of men, immediately started in pursuit. They succeeded in capturing the greater part of the marauders and in recovering $150,000 of the stolen money. The Governor-General of Canada telegraphed, offering to respond to a requisition from the United States Government for the surrender of the robbers as many of them as could be found. The raid was followed by considerable excitement, and in a few hours the whole frontier was under arms.*

The sensational story began a six-month concentration in the media, both in the States and abroad, focusing on the St. Albans raiders. From October 1864 and well into 1865, there were over 2 million newspapers articles featuring updates on the St. Albans Raid. Not all the facts were accurate, but the fear and terror had spread across the Northern states.

Chapter 16

IN THEIR OWN WORDS

Eyewitnesses shared their experiences and perspective when they wrote to friends and family to let them know of their welfare after the St. Albans Raid hit the news. Mothers and fathers were writing their soldier sons on the Union fronts to assure them that all was well. Hundreds of newspaper articles were written as the story unfolded. Unfortunately, details became blurred from the actual facts, something that was bound to happen with the limited communication systems of the day. The best records of the raid are firsthand accounts from those who experienced it. Their letters, diaries and personal accounts are priceless and timeless because they give us the story from those who were there.

The wife of Governor John G. Smith, Ann Eliza Brainerd Smith, defended their home and estate during the raid. After the raid, she was given the title of brevet general for her bravery and self-sufficiency in the midst of the crisis. Ann wrote to her husband the morning after the raid to assure him that the family was fine and that he should stay in Montpelier to do his duty. Her strength and quick thinking are obvious in her letter:

Thurs Morn, Oct. 20, 1864

My Dearest—

We have had (to use Cousin Joe's forcible expression) a "Raid from hell!"
For about half an hour yesterday afternoon I thought that we should be

Ann Eliza Brainerd Smith, wife of Vermont governor John Gregory Smith, protected her home and family when the alert of the raid was sounded. She provided weapons to local men and kept vigilant, waiting for further repercussions of the raid. Before the raid, Ann had received a visit from Bennett Young, who claimed he was a theology student, and had given him a tour of the stables and the estate. *Photo from* Images of America: St. Albans, *by L. Louise Haynes and Charlotte Pedersen with the St. Albans Historical Museum. Photo Courtesy of the St. Albans Historical Society and Museum.*

burnt up, and robbed. William gone to B___ and Ed, Mr. Inglis and Joe and Eddie up to Warner's with the apples—but I hope you don't imagine I was one moment frightened, though the noise of guns, the agitated looks of the rushing men, and our powerless condition were startling enough. I ordered the house shut and locked, hunting myself for weapons, but nothing could be found but your carved pistol _empty_. However, with that in my hand I stood in the door feeling _enraged_ but _defiant_. In a few minutes Stewart—pale enough, galloped up, and asked for arms. I gave the pistol and he told me they had turned north, but were expected back on the Sheldon road.

A number of pickets ran onto Aldis hill, where they could see, and blazed away every few minutes to let the raiders know they were in readiness. After Stewart left, we found the rifle, and I started down street to give it to somebody, but in a moment I met a man who said he was after it. We then found another pistol, and in a few moments some men rushed in to the back yard for horses, I gave Mr. Beeman factory; Major. Ed who had just got in from the cider mill (I feared the horses and all were captured) took Kitty, and two others took the team horses.

Afterwards two others took Nellie and Diamond. Diamond soon came back badly scratched, by stepping through a bridge. The man took good care of him, and William came on mail train, says he is not much hurt. The other horses are still out. Worthy has just been in, he will tell you all the news.

I worried very much about you, thought you would suffer great anxiety on our account, but my dear, never after this, think that I shall be frightened or that I cannot do all that my best judgment dictates. That may be worthless, but it will probably be in active exercise.

I expected you and got Lawrence to meet you with a team; we had nobody here then to go, but finding by William that you did not come, I saw all secure, and went to bed and slept soundly till morning, feeling that the Almighty Watcher was near me. How foolish and frantic our people have been not to heed your warning. I hope this affair will settle matters at once. Good bye. God give you grace to act wisely in these trying times.

[The following was written at the top of the first page of the letter:] William, when he heard the rumor in B., groaned, "Oh my God! The horses are gone!!!" and ran to the depot. Our little Ed's spirit was superb. While Julie and some of the rest were crying terribly, he was awfully mad. "What did you let that rifle go for?" says he to me. "It is the only thing in the house that I can use!!"

Andrew Craig Fletcher was living in St. Albans and witnessed the raid. Fletcher was nearly shot when a bullet came within a foot of him during all the shooting on Main Street. He wrote his parents, Andrew and Ruth Fletcher, the day after the raid:

> *Still Remembered Parents: I now take my Pen in hand to inform you that I am well and unhurt although one ball struck within one foot of me… Yesterday about one o'clock a party of robbers & horse thieves came into town and arrested a number of citizens to prevent giving alarm…entered all the banks took what money their* [sic] *was in them and then proceeded to the livery stables and took what horses they could find…stoped* [sic] *men on the street and took their horses away from them. What will be the result I can not tell. Tell father that if he has any St. Albans money to get rid of it as soon as possible…it is only worth 50* [cents] *on a* [dollar]. *There is no trade in town…it is all excitement.*

The night of the raid, Ann Pierce of St. Albans sat down to write her son Marshall Pierce, who was in Boston, about the event. Pierce was worried that her son would be hearing about the raid through the newspapers, so she wanted to assure him that she was safe. The two posses of local men had not returned, so St. Albanians didn't know what had become of them. Pierce stayed in her home but heard the train whistle as she penned the letter. Since the trains had been shut down by the governor after the raid, a train arriving at the depot meant the troops from Burlington were arriving and that she could go to bed knowing St. Albans was protected.

Pierce wrote:

> *Marshall, My very dear son*
>
> *I am feeling to night as I never felt before in my life. this day seems to bee the begining of trouble in St. Albans and the Lord knows when it will end, their* [sic] *was a band of men appeared in the streets…all at once comenced their awfull work…they called themselves Confedret Oficers, Devil oficers I should think. our men were runing in great confusion to colect what arms they could…*

Pierce continued with a lengthy description of the events of the raid that she had learned from friends and family who had witnessed it on Main Street:

what will become of them this dark dark night we know not. they start[ed] off in the direction of Sheldon...they threatned the town and said they had more men not far off we have sent for Arms and men to Burlington & Vergens...their is great excitement we will not go to bed to night...I now here the train whistle...I hope it is the soldiers or the Arms or something...we fear ther is others that will rise up when our men and guns are gone but we hope for the best and trust in the Lord. I just heard...the soldiers have come from Burlington...

Susan Hubbell Seymour wrote to her niece Isa C. Mygatt, of Chazy, New York, on October 20 about the incredible events that had occurred the day before. Seymour wrote that she had heard lots of shooting outdoors when she was in her house and that her servant went out to see what was happening:

Opposite here they fired twice so that my woman ran out—supposing some one was killing cats! She ran to the gate and asked them why they were firing, they laughed and rode on. She came rushing in and told me, and the serving-girl and we rushed out, bareheaded and in the rain. All the neighbors were out, and I flew over to Miranda [Mrs. F.S. Stranahan] who looked the most war-like as she was giving some directions to a man with a gun! She told me some 30 men had suddenly risen up—armed to the teeth, had robbed all the banks of all of their money, stolen all the horses in the livery stables and were off for Canada. She said they had fired and killed Mr. Morrison, the master builder of the hotel—had shot Collins Huntington while peaceably riding in his wagon—shot a woman, Mrs. Watson, &c. &c...At Miss Beattie's I found Julius and Neo [Edmund Seymour] examining the blood spots where Mr. Morrison was shot, poor man! It seems the rebels were taking horses off from a team in the road; one of his workmen and he remonstrated, whereupon he shot him. The ball entered his hand and through his abdomen...

Seymour continued:

As school was just out I of course thought of my boys, so Mrs. Fay and I went immediately down town, and Oh! what an excitement! I met Will Whiting the, first one cantering off through the mud (without any gun), then Stewart [Colonel F.S. Stranahan] then five more and so on all the way down. We women began to remonstrate that all the men and arms should not go and leave us unprotected—it was suggested perhaps they wanted to draw them off purposely so they could go on stealing unmolested…but our fears were quieted by hearing that they had telegraphed to Burlington for a military force of some 60 men.

EYEWITNESS REPORTS

At the Elinus Morrison inquest, on October 21, 1864, Myron Wilson of St. Albans testified that he was in the center office of the *St. Albans Messenger* when his son, who was at the front of the building, hollered, "There are horse thieves in the street." Wilson said, "I went to the window overlooking Main Street and saw a band of men opposite the offices and on either side of it—some on horseback, some on foot—engaged in unhitching horses attached to vehicles and fastened at the posts on the street. There appeared to be 15 or 20 men armed with revolvers from 12 to 15 inches long."

Wilson then went outside, where he saw a man standing with a small group of men and talking with a man on horseback holding a pistol. The armed man ordered the men inside, saying, "You go back into the building, and you are all right. You don't know what's going on in this country. Remember Sherman." Wilson added:

> *After they stopped, I saw Mr. Elinus J. Morrison on the steps of Miss Beattie's Millinery Shop about eight feet from me. I then saw one of the horsemen aim a pistol and fire a shot which took effect in the body of said Morrison. Morrison, after the pistol shot struck him, came off the steps and leaned against the corner of the building in a crouching position, and I said to him, "Are you hurt?" I saw the blood coming from one of his hands. Said he, "Yes, they have shot me through the body."*

Wilson was one of the men who helped carry Morrison to L.L. Dutcher's drugstore. Morrison was then moved to the American Hotel, where he died two days later.

Students and staff at St. Albans Academy also experienced the fear and terror of the raid, uncertain of what would happen to them or the town. Teacher Cora Burgess Wood and students Mary Barker, James Record, Henry Austin and John Branch Sr. all witnessed parts of the raid through school windows and wrote accounts. Wood recalled:

$10,000 REWARD!

The St. ALBANS BANK and THE FIRST NATIONAL BANK of St. Albans, Vt. were robbed by an armed band of raiders, on the 19th Oct. 1864, of the following notes and bank bills, viz:

4 1000's U. S. 7 3-10 Treasury Notes, Nos. 18681 to 18684, inclusive.
20 500's   do   Nos. 28083 to 28101, inclusive; and also 1715.
100 100's   do   Nos. 184,073 to 184,172, inclusive; and also Nos. 142.563; 145.574.
106 50's   do   Nos. 16285 to 16296, inclusive; 20,587 to 20,640, inclusive.
          30,088 to 30,096, inclusive; 134,960 to 134,980, inclusive.
          and also Nos. 20,645 and 20,646; also, 20,665 to 20,675, inclusive, and No. 32,981.
And also 6 1881 bonds, payable to L. Sowles, Cashier, or bearer, 7,927 to 7,932.

All payable to blank, order; all dated August 15, 1864. Also, $10,000 5 per cent. legal tender coupon U. S. Notes, dated December 1, 1863, with one coupon taken off, of the denominations of 50s and 100's. Also, $4,000 5 per cent. U. S. interest bearing notes. Also, $1,000 6 per cent. compound interest notes. Also, $9,000 in St. Albans and Franklin County Bank Bills and Greenbacks, and some other New England Bills.
$19,000 U. S. Legal Tenders. 4,000 do do interest bearing notes 10s, 20s, 50s, and 100's. Four $500 6 per ct. compound inst. notes. 8000 New England Bank bills. 5000 N. Y. State bank bills.
All persons are hereby cautioned against purchasing any of the above described Government notes, as payment has been stopped by the U. S. Government. The above reward will be paid for the return of the same to S. Browning, Esq., Ottawa Hotel, Montreal, C. E., or to the undersigned, and no questions will be asked, and no names disclosed. A just proportion of the above reward will be paid to any person who will return any part of the above described notes and bills, not already in the hands of the Canadian authorities.

H. R. SOWLES, President St. Albans Bank.

HIRAM BELLOWS, President First National Bank.

St. Albans, Vt., October 26, 1864.

The $10,000 reward poster that was issued on October 26, 1864, for the arrest and return of the money stolen from the St. Albans banks. St. Albans Bank president H.R. Sowles and First National Bank president Hiram Bellows issued the reward. *Courtesy of the Vermont Historical Society.*

My room on the first floor was occupied by seventy boys and girls from eight to ten years of age. Mr. Dorsey Taylor, then Principal of the School, introduced the custom of having rhetorical exercises in the hall on the third floor…the entire School assembled as usual at two o'clock on the day of the Raid. Mr. Taylor was on the platform speaking in a happy mood before the pupils when he was interrupted by a call at the door…When Mr. Taylor returned to the platform he was pale and greatly agitated. He consulted his assistants. As he looked down on the school his eyes rested on the little ones and he said, "Little dears, wicked men have done very bad things here. Now do as you are told. Go down the stairs quietly to your rooms." Having been led to believe the town was to be burned, naturally the responsibility of the children caused him great anxiety…

Wood said that after she left school, "As I walked through the park on my way home I met a stranger, to whom I said, 'Sir, can you tell me what has happened here?' He replied, 'Why, haven't you heard that men came in here and robbed our banks—and rode away on horses, taken from the streets, and are now well on their way to Canada?'"

James Record was a student of Burgess's and wrote of his recollection of the raid:

It was the custom for the classes to meet on certain days in the Assembly Room on the upper floor of the building for exercises. It was on one of these days, Wednesday, October 19, that the St. Albans raid took place. The entire school was assembled and the program had commenced when parents much excited began calling for their children. In a short time the whole room was in a frenzy of excitement. I realized that something unusual was happening but had no idea what it was. The Principal and teachers succeeded in maintaining something like order and prevented what might have been a serious panic. Calls by the parents for their children became more frequent, and in a short time the exercises were terminated and we were all marched down to the main floor and dismissed. On reaching the entrance I bolted down the steps to the street, which was filled with people hurrying in all directions. During the raid all citizens who were on the street were ordered into the park in front of the Academy, and a failure to comply promptly brought forth a fusillade of revolver shots. One person was killed and, as I remember, several were wounded. By the time I reached the streets the raiders had seized a large sum of money from the banks, appropriated horses and departed and a posse was already in pursuit. I hurried home and then to a residence being constructed a short distance north of the Academy where my father was employed. Groups of horsemen were dashing by and it seemed to me that about every able bodied man who owned a horse had joined in the chase. The raiders were pursued across the line into Canada and captured on Canadian soil and turned over to the authorities together with the money which they had stolen.

On vacation in St. Albans, J.B. Baldwin, train conductor out of Rouses Point, New York, was present when the raid occurred. He shared his eyewitness account with the *Troy Times*, and it was published the day after the raid. Following are excerpts from that article as reprinted in the *Cleveland Daily Leader* on October 24:

Mr. Baldwin had been taking a vacation for a few days—stopping at the American Hotel, St. Albans. About a week ago, some strangers came to board at this house and the Tremont. One of them, calling himself a colonel, appeared to be a prominent one among them. He was a man of medium size, about thirty-five years of age, and appeared to have no other name than that of colonel. Others of the party, who subsequently proved to be thieves and murderers, were habited in the uniform of United States officers, and all wore a sort of wrapper or cape, and each carried a satchel slung by a shoulder strap at the left side, after the manner of English sportsmen. There seemed to be no concert of action between any of these men—they said nothing to each other in public—no conversations ensued that would attract attention—to all appearances, they were substitute brokers, contractors or speculators, such as are often seen in frontier towns—St. Albans being only sixteen miles from the Canada line. On Tuesday night, the strangers in the village were reinforced by others, who arrived on the train from Rouse's Point, and new faces appeared at the breakfast tables of the hotels. On Wednesday morning, a further batch of conspirators arrived, till about thirty raiders had collected. And then the plot was ripe for execution.

Baldwin was standing on the steps of the American Hotel, "just as the town bell rang out the hour of three o'clock, when I saw a man coming out of the door of the First National Bank, and as he did so a citizen on the steps knocked him down. A second was also floored, but the third raider had a pistol in his hand, and the citizens retreated. The conductor thought the affair was the freak of some drunken men, but he soon saw symptoms of a disturbance at other points. Men appeared to be rushing about with pistols, in parties of from five to ten."

Souvenir bullets from the St. Albans Raid that have oxidized over time. *Courtesy of St. Albans Historical Society and Museum. Photo by Michelle Arnosky Sherburne.*

The raiders carried extra cylinders like the one pictured here during the St. Albans Raid. *Courtesy of St. Albans Historical Society and Museum. Photo by Michelle Arnosky Sherburne.*

Springfield, Vermont resident Clark A. Corliss was nine years old when the raid occurred. He and his grandfather had traveled to St. Albans to sell vegetables. Corliss wrote:

> *On the morning of that day, my grandfather, the late William Eaton, went to St. Albans with a double wagonload of vegetables. He unloaded his supplies and took his team to the sheds at Fowler's livery stable, then returned to do his trading. All at once the town was thrown into a commotion. There were armed men at every street ordering people to go onto the green, and men were stationed there to keep guard. All obeyed orders. Then at 2 p.m., robbers went into the St. Albans banks and ordered the cashiers of each bank to hand out the money. They did so without arguing as they thought it better to be living cowards than dead heroes. The robbers got over $200,000 and they killed one man by the name of Morrison. After the raiders left town, my grandfather thought he had better go home. He went after his team and found that the wagon and harness, minus the bridles, were left. The marauders rode the horses to Canada…My father went to Canada and got the horses, but they had been ridden so hard that they were not much good. After this raid there was a home guard of some 300 men organized, but the next spring, that company disbanded.*

The raid interrupted a Champlain Masonic chapter of the No. 1 RAM ceremony, and the secretary of the chapter, William Bridges, recorded in the October 19 chapter meeting minutes why member J.M. Wilcox was not given his Past Master degree that day:

> *Being about to confer the degree of Past Master upon Brother Wilcox, when Satan, the Prince of Devils, commenced a raid upon the banks of St. Albans (money being the root of all evil) and robbed them of many thousands of dollars. About 20 of the infernal Imps of the lower regions, cut and covered with impunity, killed Mr. Morrison, a worthy citizen, which created a great excitement in our quiet village for a half hour, until the troops of his Satanic Majesty had departed.*

News of the raid reached soldiers on the front, who became angry and wished they were back home to help protect their families. Having read the newspaper accounts, Private Isaac N. Watts of Peacham, serving with the First Vermont Artillery at Fort Slocum, guarding Washington, D.C., wrote about the raid in his diary and also to his sister: "November 2, Wednesday,

1864. No news to day till the train got in rations, mail, clothing and sutlers. Heard tonight of the rebel raid in Vt. Should like to have been there and helped straighten them out. They need the old Vt. Brig. to settle those matters." In a November 5 letter to his sister Alice M. Watts, Isaac wrote from Strasburg, Virginia: "They seem to have had quite a time at St. Albans. I wish any one of the Vt. Regt. could have been there. It would have done me good to fight the scamps."

Chapter 17
REIGN OF TERROR

The first reaction after the raiders took off out of town was shock. Susan Hubbell Seymour wrote to her niece, stating that "all along the street were squads of men, groups of ladies and school children—some crying and all looking pale, cold and frightened." Then, fear set in because they didn't know if more raiders would attack their town. They felt vulnerable and helpless when the men of town took off in two posses. But their fears were calmed when troops began arriving to guard the town.

A sentinel was immediately stationed in front of the St. Albans Court House, and the returned posse members were on guard on the Village Green. The night of the raid, Lieutenant Colonel R.C. Benton, stationed in St. Albans, reported that a stranger had been located in town and was being held overnight. He thought the suspicious person could have been a raider. But there was no proof, and the man was free to go the following morning.

The raider invasion placed Vermont in a state of emergency, and life changed drastically for Vermonters. All the Northern states on the Canadian border were afraid that the troops would come in from the north and attack. It was believed that St. Albans was the first of a wave of terrorist attacks. Ammunition, cannons and armaments were delivered to St. Albans. The home guards drilled and exercised every day on the Village Green. St. Albans became a war camp. The reign of terror had begun.

Adding to the war zone atmosphere, newspapers sent reporters from cities like Boston, New York City, Montreal and Toronto to get the story from the St. Albanians. St. Albans was once again flooded with strangers flocking to the "scene of the crime" to get information, interviews and updates for their newspapers. Seymour wrote, "Last night we had a street guard all night, and I assure you we feel as if we were seeing perilous times."

Women in St. Albans were outraged. Ann Pierce wrote to her son about friends and family who wished they were in town when the raiders were there to fight them, adding, "I wanted to myself." The governor's wife, Ann Smith, wrote to her husband that she wasn't afraid and was ready to fight and protect her home and family if the raiders came to their home.

Vermonters contacted relatives out of state and requested weapons be sent to them.

On the streets of St. Albans, a 9:00 p.m. curfew was issued, and if someone were found out after that time, they would have to prove who they were and why they were out. Anyone suspicious was apprehended and held until the authorities could ascertain whether he were a threat.

If families lived near a bridge or intersection, they had to add guard duty to their everyday business and home chores. Participation in guard intervals was described by Sheldon resident Oliver Cromwell Wait, who in late November wrote to his son Oliver Edmund Wait, then serving with the Tenth Vermont Infantry:

> We have had a guard at this Bridge commencing the night before Election. I have with Mother's & Libbe's help watched the Bridge 12 half nights… Payson Adams the other part of the night. The Capt of the Company & and one of the selectmen have been here today & made different arrangements. There is to be three & I have the care of it & watch till 10 o'clock, the other two till 6 in the morning…You see this takes up our attention now…I suppose you are as busy as we are, but you see I cannot be away over night.

From St. Albans, Andrew Fletcher wrote to his family on December 4 that there had been approximately eight suspicious people arrested and held until they could provide information about why they were in town. St. Albans, which had been a hub of travelers, marketers and strangers, was now suspicious of every unknown person on the street.

Rumors were rampant throughout Vermont and New England that more raids would come. With November approaching and the presidential election on the horizon, the northern frontier was wary that a larger raid was planned for that day. It was thought that the St. Albans Raid was only the preliminary attack.

Northerners were worried that Canada was harboring thousands of Confederate refugees, former prisoners of war and army deserters who would use the St. Albans Raid as an example and attempt their own attacks for personal gain.

The *New York Times* ran a detailed article on October 30 about possible raids over the northern border. It was articles like these that caused rumors about more raids to circulate:

> *Satisfactory information has been received by the Major-General [Dix] commanding, that rebel agents in Canada design to send into the United States, and colonize, at different points, large numbers of refugees, deserters and enemies of the Government, with a view to vote at the approaching Presidential election; and it is not unlikely, when this service to the rebel cause has been performed, that they may be organized for the purpose of shooting down peaceable citizens and plundering private property, as in the recent predatory incursions on the Detroit and at St. Albans.*

St. Albans judge James Davis's diary entry for October 24, 1864, made reference to the rumors: "It is suspected there are several thousand Southern rebels in Canada ready to come out and plunder and burn our villages whenever opportunity presents."

Edward Sowles shed light on the prevailing fear, adding that a "reign of terror" had hit Vermont:

> *It spread with the rapidity of lightning throughout the land, and threw consternation into homes and villages along the entire northern frontier, contiguous to the Provinces of Canada, and especially on the northern border of Vermont...It was the prevailing opinion that these marauders were but the advance guards of an army from Canada, which had, by surprise or collusion, temporarily overpowered their local government, and were marching through our State carrying all the horrors of war to our homes and firesides.*

Rumors were flying around the Northern states that a large army would descend on the North, and in reaction, militias were formed everywhere from Buffalo, New York, to Detroit, Michigan, and spent October and into the winter on patrol.

Vermonters were suspicious and wary of strangers. It was not believed that St. Albans was an isolated incident. People felt that another raid could happen anywhere in the state and were thus on guard.

Ben Dewey, a bank clerk in Waterbury, Vermont, wrote to his friend Colonel William Wells, off at war, on November 5:

I want you to seize for me a Spencer rifle. Confiscate and bring it home to me—Do not know that any of the hounds have made me a visit yet, though on the day of the St Albans raid I had a suspicious customer…who was visiting banks for the purpose of teaching them to detect counterfeit money. I didn't see it, and consequently he remained on the other side of the counter.

Nothing could be assumed, and safety had to be the priority. Anyone could be a Confederate in disguise or one of the escaped raiders on the lam. Just outside of St. Albans, an incident occurred in which a sniper or snipers were hiding out before being discovered by a Union soldier. The *St. Albans Messenger* ran the story in its November 28 issue, and it was picked up by the *Caledonian* in St. Johnsbury, Vermont, a few weeks later. The story reported:

One morning a boy left the house to check on mink traps in a marsh about a mile from home. While checking the traps, the boy was shot at. There was an old potato storehouse near the marsh, and shots came from there. A bullet brazed his coat, which was an old Union sergeant's coat, and one went through his cap. Thinking it was his brother messing around, the boy yelled and ran home.

The brother was actually at home, and when the boy told the story, the brother and some friends decided it must be a Rebel sniper hiding out. The boys investigated the storehouse and found signs that people had recently been staying in the outbuilding, but were gone.

If the would-be assassins were rebel emissaries, the only probable reason for thus disclosing themselves may be found in the fact that the boy wore a sergeant's coat and they might have supposed that the "boys in blue" were after them.

Chapter 18

VERMONT'S STATE MILITIA FORMED

From October 20 to November 16, Vermont militia units formed on a daily basis in order to protect the state's northern border. Vermont became a police state with people of all ages volunteering to guard roads, bridges and streets and report any suspicious or unknown people to the authorities.

In response to the St. Albans Raid, the governor issued orders that every male aged eighteen to forty-five should enlist. It was amazing that the well had not run dry. Vermont towns had been paying out bounties for three war years and supplying recruits every time the order came. Vermonters were ready to defend their own. Even if the veteran soldiers were back home from their service on the war front, they were asked to be "deployed" again.

Even after the imminent threat of more attacks on the northern frontier subsided, Vermont's government knew it had to stay prepared and protect its people. The Vermont General Assembly approved an act on November 22, 1864, to organize a state militia.

Vermont newspapers devoted entire pages to publishing the legislative orders concerning the "Act for Organizing the Militia." On December 9, the front page of the *Caledonian* ran the following press release issued by the secretary of state: "It is hereby enacted by the General Assembly of the State of Vermont, as follows: Each and every able-bodied male citizen of this state, between the ages of eighteen and forty-five years, except as hereinafter provided, shall be liable to perform military duty and shall be enrolled in the militia of this state." The time frame for the militia recruitment was thirty days from November 29, and those enlisted were committed to serve a term of five years unless discharged at an earlier date.

G.B. Bullard, superintendent for recruitment in St. Johnsbury East's Sixth District, stated in a December 16 article in the *Caledonian* that the town select boards were responsible for recruiting men from their towns. Bullard stressed to the selectmen that "Vermonters cannot afford the disgrace—after so noble a record on so many bloody battlefields—to be drafted to protect their own homes and property."

Judge James Davis wrote in his diary on Tuesday, October 25: "It appears that military companies have been raised and organized in all the frontier towns in this county, including St. Albans, Sheldon, and Enosburgh, and that the people in this region and throughout the State are much excited."

Lieutenant Colonel R.C. Benton was responsible for organizing over twenty commands and establishing a line of defense along the Missisquoi River. He had ordered that all boats on the river be secured and stationed guards at all bridges throughout the northern frontier. He wrote that "we felt our frontier was pretty fairly secured."

On November 5, Ben Dewey, a bank clerk in Waterbury, Vermont, shared the following about the aftereffects of the St. Albans Raid and the state of vigilance and alert the whole state was under:

> *The towns in the northern part of the state are armed, and in fact, generally the towns are taking measures to protect themselves. Our town has started a company, and we are daily expecting our arms. Revolvers have been in good demand, and a great many are carried here. The State is full of strangers prowling around with no apparent business...some arrests have been made—was told this morning that in St. Johnsbury a man was arrested who had letters upon his person by which they learned it was contemplated to pitch in there. A lot of arms passed through here this morning for Morrisville, Hyde Park and Johnson.*

Organization of Vermont's State Cavalry

Vermont's government was determined to bring order out of the sudden chaos and stood at the ready to defend its people. The state was divided into twelve military districts, each broken down to ten company districts supervised by Adjutant General P.T. Washburn. The entire state was involved, from the Canadian to the Massachusetts border and from the New York to the New Hampshire border.

The twelve districts were:

District 1: St. Albans and surrounding area
District 2: Burlington, Chittenden and Lamoille Counties
District 3: Vergennes and twenty-four surrounding towns
District 4: Montpelier and the vicinity
District 5: Albany east to Newport and south to Lyndon, Burke and Sheffield (a total of thirty-five towns)
District 6: Barnet, St. Johnsbury, Danville, Peacham, Hardwick and the area south to Topsham and Newbury and east to Concord and Lunenburg (a total of nineteen towns)
District 7: Bradford
District 8: Windsor
District 9. Rutland
District 10: Springfield
District 11: Bennington
District 12: Brattleboro

The Frontier Cavalry was a provisional force of 2,215 militiamen placed in service by the state to guard the frontier. This force was soon succeeded by veteran troops of the Invalid Corps and a cavalry organization composed of seven companies from New York, three from Massachusetts and two from Vermont. The regiment known as the Twenty-sixth New York Cavalry was directed by the New York governor and remained in New York State. The two Vermont companies, which served at Burlington and St. Albans, consisted of 101 officers and men each and were raised under authority granted by President Lincoln to General Dix, who was commanding the Department of the East. The companies were mustered into the service on January 10, 1865, at Burlington.

Throughout the state, towns were organizing their own militias. On the eastern side of Vermont, more than two hours away from St. Albans, towns in Caledonia, Orange and Windsor Counties organized units. Ryegate native Captain William Henderson, formerly of Company G, Ninth Regiment but paroled and discharged on physical disability in 1863, raised a company from Peacham, Groton and Ryegate. The *History of Ryegate, Vt.*, states, "After the St. Albans raid in 1864, a regiment of militia, composed mainly of veterans, was organized for the defense of the northern frontier, and Wm. J. Henderson of Ryegate was appointed Major. This organization was not long needed."

The *Caledonian* reported that the "Frontier Cavalry" had two companies organized "for service on the border" and that Captain Josiah Grout, General William Grout's younger brother, was the first company captain for the St. Johnsbury unit: "Capt. Grout is well known in this section, having enlisted from East St. Johnsbury, where his parents now reside. He…was severely wounded by Mosby's men, perhaps two years ago, from which wound he still suffers, the bullet never having been extracted."

The thirty-one infantry provisional companies contained 1,781 officers and men, while the fourteen cavalry provisional companies had 434 officers and men. That totaled 2,215 soldiers guarding and patrolling the state.

The breakdown of town volunteers and provisional militia companies organized for the defense of the frontier against invasion from Canada were:

INFANTRY

Barton, 105

Irasburgh, 103

St. Johnsbury, 101

St. Albans, 100

Newport, 97

Burlington, 93

North Troy, 91

Lyndon, 77

Derby Line, 63

Charleston, 60

Richford, 60

Sheldon, 60

Swanton, 60

Waterbury, 53

Canaan, 45

Woodstock, 44

Highgate, 40

East Highgate, 40

Franklin, 40

East Franklin, 40

West Berkshire, 40

Berkshire Center, 40

East Berkshire, 40

Montgomery, 40

Enosburgh Falls, 40

West Enosburgh, 40

Hyde Park, 40

North Enosburgh, 39

Alburgh Springs, 30

Johnson, 30

West Alburgh, 30

CALVARY

Burlington, 60
Sheldon, 60
St. Albans, 60
Newport, 32
Barton, 31
Derby Center, 31
Irasburgh, 30

Richford, 30
St. Johnsbury, 30
Swanton, 30
Derby Line, 25
Highgate, 25
Berkshire Centre, 15
Franklin 15

By the end of December 1864, the immediate threat had dissipated, and Colonel Proctor and Lieutenant Benton were able to step down from their appointments. Major John Barstow, formerly of the Eighth Vermont Regiment, took their place.

All of Vermont's frontier militia units guarded and patrolled until they were mustered out at Burlington in June 1865. Several provisional companies had been discharged on January 20, when it was decided that their presence was no longer necessary. The remaining provisional cavalry companies were disbanded on June 1.

Part III

The Raiders' Trials in Canada

Chapter 19

POSSIBLE INTERNATIONAL INCIDENT

Once the raiders crossed the Canadian border, the United States, Great Britain and Canada were put in a very difficult situation. President Lincoln realized the precarious situation that had evolved when he learned that Americans had tried to arrest the raiders in Canada. General Dix's order to the St. Albans posse to pursue the raiders into Canada and "destroy them" broke many rules.

So, from the moment the raiders were on Canadian soil, the Americans had to tread carefully. Lincoln couldn't push any issues because the relationship between Canada–Great Britain and the United States was very tense. Great Britain didn't want to get pulled into the American Civil War. The United States could not have survived a war on top of the War of the Rebellion against the Confederacy.

An article in the *Montreal Gazette* titled "Outrage of St. Albans," published the day after the raid, addressed the duties of the Canadian government with emotions set aside:

> *It is the first duty of the Government and the people of Canada to see that the right of asylum which their soil affords is not thus betrayed and violated. The Government must spare no pains to prevent it; and it is the first duty of the inhabitants of this country, especially those who live on the borders, to give instant information of any attempt they may see to the nearest magistrate, and the duty of the magistrate immediately to inform the Government. We must, we repeat, preserve our neutrality, and their right*

of asylum which British soil affords inviolate, and punish with the sternest severity any breach which can be discovered. If we do not, we shall find ourselves dragged into the war for needless cause; our eastern frontier lit up with the fires of now peaceful homes, and the country on both sides of the line made red with murders.

The Canadian government did have to protect its own, especially with its mother country, Great Britain, watching every move.

Why was the relationship between the United States and Canada–Great Britain so bad? Well, it went back to the War of 1812. The War of 1812 was a two-and-a-half-year conflict between the United States and the United Kingdom, consisting of Great Britain, Ireland, Canada and Indian allies. The United States declared war because of trade restrictions, British support of American Indian tribes against American western expansion and a fight over the Canadian territories. The conflict did settle some issues, but there was still resentment, unsettled business and tension between the two sides.

Around 1837, French Canadians rebelled against the British government and were suppressed and defeated by imported British soldiers. Many French Canadians fled to Vermont towns like Alburg, Swanton and St. Albans, as well as to upstate New York. With the influx of these refugees, U.S. president Martin Van Buren sent troops to the border to prevent a conflict or war. Many Canadians harbored ill feelings toward the United States regarding its support of these refugees.

Britain was not happy about the immigration of its people to America during the 1830s and 1840s. Tens of thousands of Brits moved to the States because it was the "land of opportunity." Half of the American territory was just beginning to be settled, so there was plenty of free land to be had. Brits could start fresh and capitalize on the western expansion, as well as the industries and businesses that were growing in the East. Brits saw the benefit of success and opportunity "across the pond."

The British also resented the United States because they knew that because there were no copyright laws in the nineteenth century, Americans were benefitting freely from plagiarizing and reprinting British literary works. It got so bad that fifty-six English authors eventually pushed for copyright legislation because there was no protection of their work and Americans were publishing whatever they found.

On both sides, money was an issue. Americans had borrowed approximately $150 million from Great Britain by 1839. The United States was experiencing major growth and needed financial backing, and the former mother country could afford to give the aid. But the love-hate relationship that is common between borrowers and lenders added to Americans' resentment.

In the 1840s, the slave trade was at its peak, and America's South was the largest recipient of slaves. Britain had abolished slavery, and according to Thomas A. Bailey in *A Diplomatic History of the American People*, "friction over the African slave trade was likewise generating heat. The British, in an effort to halt this odious traffic, were attempting to establish a right to search American merchant ships in time of peace." This offended Americans, who didn't want to give any more rights to the British.

The border between the United States and Canada was a major bone of contention from 1812 on. Arguments about Maine, Minnesota and Oregon were bitter, and it took a long time to negotiate and settle who owned what. Due to these border disputes, two men—U.S. secretary of state Daniel Webster and British diplomat Lord Alexander Ashburton—were commissioned to negotiate a treaty. They worked tirelessly, and the result was the Webster-Ashburton Treaty.

The Webster-Ashburton Treaty, signed on August 9, 1842, resolved many disputed issues in British-American relations during the mid-nineteenth century. Of these, boundary disputes were the most prominent. After the War of 1812, the United States complained that Britain still habitually violated American sovereignty. The dispute over the northeastern boundary, between Maine and New Brunswick, Canada, had brought nationals of the two countries to the verge of armed hostility. The treaty settled this through what then appeared to be a wise compromise of territorial claims providing the present-day boundary line.

The treaty also rectified the U.S.-Canada boundary at the head of the Connecticut River, at the north end of Lake Champlain, on the Detroit River and at the head of Lake Superior. An article about free navigation of the St. John River was included in the treaty. Additionally, the United States was issued protection against British search of American vessels in regard to the slave trade.

The part of the Webster-Ashburton Treaty that would play a large role in the St. Albans raiders' trials was the article about extradition. Article 10 stated:

> It is agreed that the United States and Her Britannic Majesty shall…deliver up to justice, all persons who, being charged with the crime of murder, or assault with intent to commit murder, or piracy, or arson, or robbery, or forgery, or the utterance of forged paper, committed within the jurisdiction of either, shall seek an asylum, or shall be found, within the territories

of the other; provided that this shall only be done upon such evidence of criminality as, according to the laws of the place where the fugitive or person so charged shall be found...and if, on such hearing, the evidence be deemed sufficient to sustain the charge, it shall be the duty of the examining Judge or Magistrate to certify the same to the proper Executive Authority, that a warrant may issue for the surrender of such fugitive.

Even with the Webster-Ashburton Treaty, the tension was thick, and the United States had to tread carefully.

Chapter 20

Trial One:
The St. Albans Bank Case

The world was watching when the St. Albans raiders' trial began on October 24, 1864. For six months, the newspapers updated readers of the trial's progress.

Newspapers from all over the United States, Canada and abroad ran articles on the trial. The *St. Albans Messenger* had a reporter on the scene and kept everyone back home informed of the daily proceedings. However, it also commented that the *Montreal Evening Telegraph* was "a secesh institution" and sarcastically reported that "the case is in able hands…it is pleasing to remark that thus far the acts of the Canadian authorities are all that could be desired in the case." Obviously, the *Messenger* was a bit biased.

The first hearing was held at St. Johns on October 24, 1864, with Judge Charles Coursol presiding. But the raiders' defense team was not ready. As published in the *New York Times* on October 26, "Nothing of special importance has taken place in regard to the St. Albans, Vt., raiders since my last account…The notorious George N. Sanders is here, managing the cause of the rebels. He says they belong to the first families of Kentucky, and formerly belonged to John Morgan's forces. This raid, he asserts, is only the first of a series of plundering expeditions soon to take place on the frontiers of the lakes."

The defense team was assembled by Sanders and consisted of John J.C. Abbott, former solicitor general and dean of McGill University Law School; T.A. Rodolphe LaFlamme, a criminal lawyer; and William Kerr, defense attorney. It was recorded in the CSA war records on an expense sheet for

Lieutenant Bennett Young that over $6,000, in the care of George and his son Lewis Sanders, was allotted on October 22 for the defense of the raiders.

On the urging of Sanders and the Confederates, Coursol decided to move the trial to Montreal because St. Johns was too close to the American border and within reach of angry Vermonters who had been arriving in St. Johns for depositions. Rumors circulated that Americans would try to kidnap the raiders or that Confederate sympathizers would do the same. Sanders promoted these rumors and also the fact that the Americans had put Canada at risk by attempting to capture the raiders on foreign territory. The public's outrage intensified when it learned of the October 19 orders from General John Dix to ignore the border line and pursue no matter what.

The Confederates won a minor battle in the court system when the prisoners were transferred by train to Montreal on October 27. Everything changed for the raiders in Montreal. They were received like heroes by prominent citizens, dignitaries, city officials and even the mayor. They were festively paraded in a convoy of carriages with crowds of supporters lining the streets to get a glimpse of the famous raiders. They arrived at Au Pied du Courant, the Montreal jail, but were given apartments, not cells. The *St. Albans Messenger* reported that "they were wined and dined and treated like royalty." Sanders put his son Lewis in charge of ensuring that the men had everything they wanted. No prison cells, no rats, no sleeping on cold floors with no blankets, no rations unfit for pigs—it was not the usual nineteenth-century jail scene for these raiders. They had prominent Montreal citizens, dignitaries, government officials and Confederate sympathizers visiting.

On October 26, George Sanders wrote the following to the *Evening Telegraph* in Montreal, testifying on behalf of the raiders:

> *I cannot permit the many unfounded statements in regards to the Confederate attack upon St. Albans to pass without a word of explanation as to the facts. The attack upon St. Albans was made by Confederate soldiers, under the command of Lieut. Bennett H. Young, of the C.S.A., all having served in the Confederate army within the Confederate states, and being still in the service, were especially commissioned and detailed for that service, under the direct authority of, and, in fact, by direct order from the Government of the Confederate States.*

Sanders also stressed that the soldiers made public declarations of their status and intentions and that they were acting "under orders of the Southern Confederacy."

The raiders and Reverend Stephen Cameron on the steps of the Montreal jail, December 27, 1864. *Front row, left to right*: Lieutenant Bennett Young, William Hutchinson Huntley and Marcus Spurr. *Back row, left to right*: Charles Swagar, Reverend Stephen Cameron and Squire Turner Tevis. *Courtesy of the William Notman Photographic Collection, McCord Museum.*

Secretary of State William Seward had issued on October 21 a demand for the extradition of the fugitives so they could be prosecuted in the United States under the Webster-Ashburton Treaty.

Even before the trial began, Confederate commissioner Clement Clay reported to Judah Benjamin, secretary of state for the CSA, on November 1 that the majority of Canadians were on the side of the raiders.

On November 2, 1864, the trial called the "St. Albans Bank Case" began in the Montreal Police Court with Judge Charles Coursol residing. The prosecution team consisted of Bernard Devlin representing the U.S. government with the assistance of John Rose. State Supreme Court justice Asa Aldis, Henry Edson and U.S. senator George Edmunds represented the state of Vermont, and lawyer Edward Sowles represented the St. Albans banks. For the British government and Crown, Francis Jonson, Stephen Bethune and Edward Carter were the representatives.

The first hurdle of the trial was to get past the authority and jurisdiction. The defense attorney applied for a writ of habeas corpus claiming that Judge Coursol was not authorized to oversee the trial and that he had gone beyond his jurisdiction already. It was eventually decided that Coursol was within his jurisdiction, and the trial proceeded.

The accused fourteen men were charged with assault against Cyrus Bishop and stealing property of the St. Albans Bank. Instead of facing charges relating to all three banks and all of the citizens of St. Albans, the charges were pared down to two specific ones. If the raiders had been on trial in the United States, all of those charges would have been addressed.

On November 9, a warrant was delivered to the court from Franklin County justice of the peace Leonard Gilman. It stated:

> *By the authority of the State of Vermont, you are hereby commanded to apprehend the bodies of the said Samuel Eugene Lackey, Thomas Bronsdon Collins, Squire Turner Tevis, Alamanda Pope Bruce, Marcus Spurr, William H. Hutchinson, Charles Moore Swagar, Bennett H. Young, George Scott, Caleb McDowall Wallace, James Alexander Doty, Joseph McGrorty, Samuel Simpson Gregg and Dudley Moore…and them have before me at the office of the sheriff in St. Albans, aforesaid, there and then to answer unto the foregoing complaint, and to be further dealt with according to law.*

The Vermont warrant was issued by Franklin County court clerk Joseph Brainerd, Supreme Court judge Asa Aldis and Governor Smith. The charges were the State of Vermont vs. all of the abovementioned men.

The warrant also stated that the accused had caused "bodily harm, assault…feloniously and violently did rob, steal, take, and carry away, contrary to form, force, and effect of statute of said state."

This photo of some of the apprehended raiders was taken in the Montreal jail office in February 1864. *Front row, left to right*: William Hutchinson Huntley, Marcus Spurr and Lieutenant Bennett Young. *Back row, left to right*: Reverend Stephen Cameron, who was sent by Confederate commissioners to aid the raiders; George Scott or Charles Swagar (identifications differ in different sources); and Squire Turner Tevis. *Courtesy of the University of Vermont Libraries, Special Collections, Bailey/Howe Library.*

In the Montreal courts, the Vermont warrant didn't have any authority.

The trial continued with the witness testimony of numerous St. Albans citizens and Canadian law enforcement involved with the arrests. One of the main points pushed by the prosecution was that according to the witnesses' testimony, the accused wore civilian clothes and not uniforms. This meant that they could not have been properly identified as Confederate soldiers by the citizens of St. Albans.

After the witnesses testified, the fourteen suspects were allowed to give statements beginning on November 12. Court record states: "Voluntary Statement of the Prisoners charged before the Judge of the Sessions, with having on the 19th October last, at St. Albans, in the State of Vermont, one of the United States of America, feloniously assaulted and put in fear of his life, and stolen from one Cyrus Newton Bishop, the sum of $70,000 current money of the United States."

The first voluntary statement was from Lieutenant Young. Each of the accused gave very similar statements and accounts. But Young acted as a true commander of his military unit by defending them as well as himself and also referring authority to his superiors, which in this case was the Confederate government. Young's statement to the court was as follows:

I am a native of Kentucky, and a citizen of the Confederate States, to which I owe allegiance. I am a commissioned officer in the army of the Confederate States, with which the United States are now at war. I owe no allegiance to the United States. I herewith produce my commission as first lieutenant in the army of the Confederate States, and also the instructions I received when that commission was conferred upon me; reserving the right to put in evidence further instructions I have received, at such time and in such manner as my counsel shall advise. Whatever was done at St. Albans was done by the authority and order of the Confederate Government. I have not violated the neutrality law of either Canada or Great Britain. Those who were with me at St. Albans were all officers, or enlisted soldiers of the Confederate army, and were then under my command. They were such before the 19th October last, and their terms of enlistment have not expired. Several of them were prisoners of war, taken in battle by the Federal forces, and retained as such, from which imprisonment they escaped. The expedition was not set on foot or projected in Canada. The course I intended to pursue in Vermont, and which I was able to carry out but partially, was to retaliate in some measure for the barbarous atrocities of Grant, Butler, Sherman, Hunter, Milroy, Sheridan, Grierson, and other Yankee officers, except that I would scorn to harm women and children under any provocation, or unarmed, defenceless, and unresisting citizens, even Yankees, or to plunder for my own private benefit. I am not prepared for the full defence of myself and my command, without communication with my Government at Richmond; and insomuch as such communication is interdicted by the Yankee Government, by land and by sea, I do not think I can be ready for such full defence under thirty days, during which time I hope to be able to obtain material and important testimony without the consent of said Yankee Government, from Richmond.

Entered into evidence were the commissions and orders Young had received from the Confederate government and Secretary of War James Seddon in regards to the mission. One of the pieces of evidence was his commission of first lieutenant of the Provisional Army on June 16, 1864, issued by Secretary of War Seddon for the Confederate States of America in Richmond.

In print, Young had proof that he was ordered to organize a group of twenty soldiers for a special mission and that the CSA would provide their pay, food, clothing and transportation. In the third commission, Seddon had stated that Young "will take care to organize within the territory of the enemy, to violate none of the neutrality laws." More importantly, Young produced a memo he received from Clement C. Clay Jr., a Confederate commissioner for the CSA, that stated:

> *Your report of your doings, under your instructions of 16th June last from the Secretary of War, covering the list of twenty Confederate soldiers who are escaped prisoners, collected and enrolled by you under these instructions, is received. Your suggestions for a raid upon accessible towns in Vermont, commencing with St. Albans, is approved, and you are authorized and required to act in conformity with that suggestion.*

After that first statement, the accused probably thought the evidence was enough to end the trial then and there. But the main question on the table was: Were the acts against the citizens and banks of St. Albans conducted by criminals for personal gain or by soldiers during wartime on authorized missions? The defense team thought it was obvious.

Even before the trial began, Commissioner Clay had warned Secretary of State Judah Benjamin that existing documents might not be enough and that "the Confederate government will consider it to be their duty to recognize officially the acts of Lieutenant Young and his party, and will find means to convey such recognition to the prisoners here, in such a form as can be proven before our courts."

Indeed, Clay had suspected correctly. Young's commission documents were not enough, and Bernard Devlin of the prosecution questioned the validity of those orders. In any case, the trial was to proceed with the remaining accused giving their statements.

The American prosecution and citizens attending the proceedings must have thought it a circus and not a real trial when the defense produced such ridiculous arguments as questioning whether the St. Albans Bank actually was a "bank." How they must have been infuriated to listen to such nonsense.

Collins and Wallace formally requested a recess and time for their defense team to obtain necessary documentation from the Confederate government. Judge Coursol called for a monthlong recess for that purpose. The trial would resume on December 13. The Confederate defense team had won a minor victory and received the delay they wanted.

The *St. Albans Messenger* ran the following comments on November 18 in regards to the recess:

> *The St. Albans Raiders are evidently in better favor with the Canadian courts than they were a fortnight since: The production of a rebel commission by the leading raider, has acted like a charm on the title loving Canadian judge, and he has agreed to a postponement of the trial till December 13…Judge Coursol in granting this request may be acting up to the strict line of his duty simply, but it looks very much as though he had a fellow-feeling for the raiders and was willing to help them all that is possible, which if it proves to be so, will not tend at all to improve the relations between the United States and Canada.*

Chapter 21
TRIAL RECESS

During the recess, the raiders enjoyed the comforts and company of Montreal's Confederate sympathizers. It was noted that Judge Coursol's daughter Mary visited Young many times during this break.

During this time, Young sent a letter to the *St. Albans Messenger* dated November 17 requesting two copies of the newspaper with trial coverage. His audacity to comment about not being able to be in St. Albans because he was otherwise engaged must have infuriated the people in St. Albans. Young wrote: "You are somewhat abusive, but I have sufficient magnanimity to overlook your ire, feeling that in after years you will do me the justice to repair the wrong." He facetiously wrote that he was currently staying at "Payette's Hotel," Payette being the name of the jailer and the "hotel" being the jail. He also paid with money stolen from one of the banks. It is interesting that he was still in possession of any personal items after being arrested—especially "stolen goods"!

In a second letter, this one to S.W. Skinner, the owner of the Tremont Hotel in St. Albans, Young wrote of his location being "Away down East in the State of Maine, Nov. 25th 1864." Young sent a five-dollar St. Albans Bank note to pay for his hotel bill. This facetious letter referenced a greeting to bank cashier Cyrus Bishop at St. Albans Bank, reminding Bishop of his sworn allegiance to the Confederacy, and also a message to the young woman he had spent time with at the Tremont. Young signed it simply "A Raider."

The reason for the trial recess was to get necessary documentation from the Confederate government. The Confederate raiders' defense team sent two

The modern-day exterior of the Au Pied-du-Courant Prison on 905 Ave de Lorimier. This prison, in use from 1835 to 1912, housed fourteen of the St. Albans raiders during their trials. The prison is located near the St. Lawrence River and Jacques-Cartier Bridge. *Courtesy of the collection of Daniel S. Rush and E. Gale Pewitt, authors of* The St. Albans Raiders.

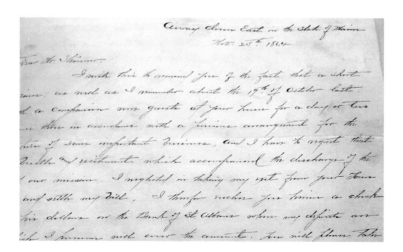

A copy of Lieutenant Young's letter to S.W. Skinner, owner of the Tremont Hotel, written while Young was imprisoned in Montreal. Young sent along stolen bank notes to settle his hotel bill and signed the letter "A Raider." *Courtesy of the Vermont Historical Society.*

messengers from Montreal to Richmond, Virginia. On the way south, one messenger was captured on November 12 by a Union agent, Major-General Christopher Augur. Augur confiscated a letter from Confederate commissioner Clement Clay to Judah Benjamin, CSA secretary of state. The letter was written on November 1, 1864, when Clay was in St. Catharine's. This letter also updated Benjamin on the Confederate sympathies in Canada.

The letter detailed the St. Albans Raid particulars from Clay's point of view. Clay wrote about his recommendations of Young prior to his commission as lieutenant and orders to travel to Canada:

> *He attempted to burn the town of St. Albans, Vermont, and would have succeeded but for the failure of the chemical preparations with which he was armed. Believing the town was already fired in several places, and must be destroyed, he then robbed the banks of all the funds he could find, amounting to more than two hundred thousand dollars.*
>
> *That he was not prompted by selfish or mercenary motives, and that he did not intend to convert the funds taken to his own use, but to that of the Confederate States, I am as well satisfied as I am that he is an honest man, a true soldier and patriot...*
>
> *He assured me before going on the raid that his efforts would be to destroy towns and farm houses, not to plunder or rob; but he said, if after firing a town, he saw he could take funds from a bank or any house which might inflict injury on the enemy and benefit his own government, he would do so.*

The messenger was held as a Union prisoner. The other messenger was Stephen F. Cameron, a Confederate chaplain who had been in Niagara Falls during the peace conference attempts and had also attended to the raiders while they were in prison. He was photographed with some of the raiders when they were in prison. Cameron was able to get through Union lines and made it to Richmond. He received the paperwork from Davis's CSA staff and worked his way north again. Ironically, Cameron chose the route from Washington, D.C., up through New England and into Vermont. Cameron, disguised as a priest traveling with two nuns, made his way through St. Albans undetected. He was successful in reaching Montreal with the documents.

Word of the difficulties of the first courier reached Montreal, so on November 18, the Confederate defense team sent a letter to President Lincoln asking for permission for a courier to pass through the Union lines. The request was accompanied by a plea from Lord Lyons on behalf of the Canadian court system asking Lincoln to "aid in giving effect to the humane decision of Judge Coursol, granting these unfortunate men a delay till the thirteenth of December to enable them to obtain evidence to be sent in their defense."

It seems that the Lincoln administration chose to ignore the request. The defense team attempted a petition to Governor General Lord Monck for assistance in this matter. But Lord Monck, "fearful of the wrath of Uncle Sam, and who were as anxious for the extradition of the prisoners as the authorities at Washington, themselves," chose not to help them, wrote Oscar Kinchen in *Daredevils of the Confederate Army*.

DISPELLING MISCONCEPTIONS OF RAIDERS

The facts about the raiders were mixed in with propaganda and misinformation. The general public in the North found it unfathomable that this event was a planned, strategic move on the part of the Confederate military. It had to be a renegade gang of bandits taking advantage of Northern citizens just for the fun of it.

As with any news story that has everyone talking, the details were blurred and became more grandiose. Although there were issues of neutrality and jurisdiction, the American public let their emotions take over. They didn't care if the raiders were Confederate soldiers. They were angry because of the way they behaved and hid their true identities. The public opinion in Canada, Europe, England and the United States was that the raid was uncivilized and handled badly by those involved. It didn't matter that Union and Confederate raids were conducted on a regular basis on Rebel territory during the Civil War. This was geographically out of the war zone and thus was not acceptable.

To dispel the tainted images of the St. Albans raiders, it is necessary to look at the facts of who these men were. They were not scallywags, ex-convicts, outlaws, marauders, land pirates, ruffians, criminals or thieves. Their motives for the raid were not selfish—they had not planned to abscond with the loot, to pillage and plunder just for the fun of it. But of course, to the citizens of St. Albans, they were all of the above, only calling themselves Confederates or soldiers. It was a bone of contention with the St. Albanians that the raiders hadn't worn uniforms or displayed themselves as soldiers. The townspeople were disgusted that they considered themselves Southern "gentlemen" and yet did not wear uniforms identifying their affiliation, carried no colors and acted like common criminals.

Vermont nineteenth-century historian Abigail Hemenway acknowledged the inaccurate reporting and impressions the public had of the St. Albans Raid in her article "Raid of '64":

> *A band of armed and desperate ruffians, in the interest of the slave-holders rebellion, 22 in number, succeeded, by a secret and well planned movement, in robbing our banks in open day-light, and in escaping to their base of operations in Canada with their plunder…An impression has gone abroad, that the raiders came into the town in a body and proceeded to make an open attack upon our citizens, intimidating them into a state of passive submission, while they were despoiling the banks of their treasure and our people of their property. This is not true.*

Even after 150 years, stories persist of a band of renegade, ex-soldiers who attacked the town and started a battle. Yes, the St. Albans Raid was the northernmost land action of the Civil War, but it was no battle, as the townspeople were caught off guard and unprotected.

There has been a discrepancy over the years of the number of raiders involved in the St. Albans Raid. Newspaper reports were inaccurate and range from twenty to fifty, but the general consensus is that there were twenty-one raiders. Young's muster roll, titled "Muster Roll of the 5th Company Confederate States of America Retributors, Lt. Young Commanding at Chicago, Illinois, Dated August 31, 1864," lists the soldiers involved, along with three extra men who didn't participate, in the St. Albans Raid.

Though the battle in the Canadian courts lasted for months, the main question was: Were the acts against the citizens and banks of St. Albans conducted by criminals for personal gain or by soldiers during wartime on authorized missions?

The interesting oversight in all the articles, eyewitness accounts, court records, letters and journal entries is the fact that Americans refused to accept that the St. Albans raiders were soldiers on a military mission.

Once they announced the raid had begun, the men repeatedly stated they were Confederate soldiers acting on orders from the Confederate government and not independently conducting the mission for personal gain. It was plain and simple. When they were announcing their intentions to the St. Albans citizens or being interrogated, arrested or questioned on the witness stand, the twenty-one Confederate soldiers remained true to their government.

Cutting through all the red tape, presiding judge on the second court case of the St. Albans raiders, Justice James Smith of the Montreal Superior Court, issued the following statement in the court records on February 14, 1865:

> [The raid was] *a hostile expedition by the Confederate States against the United States and therefore an act of war, not an offense for which extradition could be claimed. They were not robbers, but soldiers and subjects of a belligerent power, engaged in a hostile expedition against their enemy. Though the Confederate States are not recognized as independent, they are recognized as a belligerent power, and there can be do doubt that parties acting in their behalf would not be criminally responsible. It cannot be robbery, because open war exists between the two parties, and the law of nations does not regard an act of aggression by the subjects of the revolted country against the persons or property of the parent company as murder or robbery; it is a political or military act.*

TRIAL ONE BACK IN SESSION

The month of recess passed quickly, and the trial resumed on December 13. Judge Charles Coursol gave a long dissertation and then rendered a lengthy decision before any testimony could be heard. Coursol ruled: "I therefore declare that having no warrant from the Governor General to authorize the arrest of the accused, as required by the Imperial Act, I posses no jurisdiction. Consequently I am bound in law, justice and fairness to order the immediate release of the prisoners from custody upon all charges brought before me. Let the prisoners be discharged."

The courtroom erupted into celebratory chaos. Edward Sowles reported that "the final announcement of their discharge was attended with rounds of applause and screams never before heard or known in a court of justice, in which all seemed to participate." John Rose, Bernard Devlin and George Edmunds tried to protest, but the decision had been made.

There was shouting, stomping, whistling and, of course, "Rebel yells" from the raiders. After much hugging, handshaking and cheering among the Confederate sympathizers, the raiders themselves and their defense team, it was time to spread the news. Sowles wrote, "Then there was a rush for the doors and streets, and the news spread through the city and country with great celerity."

Coursol also ordered Chief of Police Guillaume Jean-Baptist Lamothe to return the funds that had been confiscated from the raiders upon their arrests. The money had already been withdrawn from the Montreal branch of the Bank of Ontario and was waiting in a court anteroom. Lamothe gave the raiders their "loot," and a quick exit was planned. Sleighs were waiting outside, ready for the exit of the raiders, who rode away from the courthouse as free men.

The shock of the decision sent waves of anger and disgust across North America and oversees. The newspaper headlines infuriated the public: "Raiders Freed! St. Albans Raiders Released!"

Reactions to Coursol's ruling in American newspapers was disgust and disappointment. The *Burlington Free Press* could not believe that the Canadian court system could allow "such a farce as this to be enacted under the name of judicial proceeding." Americans demanded answers.

The *New York Tribune* held Britain accountable for the horrible job Coursol did in the Canadian court system. The *Tribune* stated that the U.S. government should be asking the British how the ruling could be justified and if the British meant to "permit war to be waged upon the United States from her territory and by men amendable to her laws."

The media pointed out that after the raid, it was obvious that Canada was now the haven for rebels, miscreants, thieves and anti-American forces. *Walton's Journal* asked, "Will Congress take notice that a Canadian Court has done what it could to make Canada the rendezvous for robbers and incendiaries, there to arrange plots and organize bands for preying upon citizens of the United States?" It also reported that Canada had become a Confederate sanctuary and the U.S. government should treat it as "rebel ground" just like the South. The *Burlington Times* reported, "Anxiously we wait until we can reply to such an insult as we have suffered at the hands of the Canadian authorities."

Though the U.S. public and media wanted to retaliate in some form against Canada for the embarrassing debacle of the raiders' trial, Lincoln's administration knew there was eminent danger of rocking the apple cart because the Union couldn't handle a war with a second party. No matter how unjust and unfair the ruling was, even after two more trials, Americans had to accept it and move on.

When news about the release of the raiders hit Washington, Seward sent a message to the Canadian prime minister stating:

While disappointment, disgust and regret on account of the escape of the felons at Montreal are expressed by the Canadian authorities, and while the expression is believed to be sincere, yet we have no authentic information that any proceedings have been taken to vindicate the so-called neutrality of the British provinces, or prevent repetition of the injuries of which we complained, other than the unavailing renewed pursuit of the offenders out of the one colony into another. This is the condition of affairs on the other side of the boundary...It is impossible to consider those proceedings as either legal, just or friendly towards the United States.

It was a huge defeat for the Americans and especially the people of St. Albans, who had been victimized and wanted to see justice on the terrorists. Americans were at a disadvantage with the trial being in Canada, and the majority of court attendees were Confederate sympathizers.

There was no sympathy for the Americans, and they endured ridicule on the streets, in the courtroom and wherever they stayed. Americans, especially those from St. Albans, must have been furious but also deflated. How could this have happened?

As for Judge Coursol, Lord Monck made sure that an investigation into his actions was conducted. Coursol admitted that he had associated with George Sanders and John Porterfield, who was the Canadian financial agent for the Confederate government. It was rumored that Coursol had been bribed. The judge was suspended from office. Also, Chief of Police Lamothe's actions were questioned, and he was fired from his position.

The *St. Albans Messenger* reported that sources stated Coursol had admitted to being bribed. It was also insinuated that the lengthy decision he read on December 13 had been written by the defense team. Lamothe was chastised for mishandling the stolen funds by securing them from the bank for the newly released prisoners. It was thought that he acted independently, probably bribed by Confederates as well.

Also, Judge Coursol's dismissal after his ruling in the first trial showed that the Canadian-British government knew this was a piece of a larger picture and that Coursol hadn't followed the right channels. A chain of command should have been adhered to, considering the Webster-Ashburton Treaty. This situation put Canada in a precarious position with the U.S. Britain knew it, and the Canadian prime minister knew it.

Chapter 22

TRIAL TWO FOR FIVE RAIDERS

Freedom was short-lived for five of the raiders. Immediately, the U.S. prosecution filed for a new warrant to arrest the raiders for a new trial. But it took time to get any authorities to sign off on the warrant. While the Canadian authorities dragged their feet in authorizing the warrant, the raiders were getting out of Montreal quickly.

Chief of Police Lamothe refused to sign the warrant, and the U.S. prosecution was delayed until it finally convinced Superior Judge James Smith to sign it. This delay allowed the majority of the raiders to escape. Only five were recaptured and rearrested under the new warrant: Young, Squire Tevis, Spurr, Hutchinson and Swagar. These raiders were arrested on December 20. The world's focus returned to Montreal with the news that the second raider trial would begin on December 27.

The proceedings on record were before Judge Smith and stated:

> *Immediately after the discharge of the prisoners by Judge Coursol, Mr. Justice Smith issued a warrant for the re-arrest of the prisoners, similar to those under which they had been previously in custody. On this warrant, five out of the thirteen, namely Lieutenant Bennett H. Young, W.H. Hutchinson, Squire Turner Tevis, Charles Moore Swagar, and Marcus Spurr, were again arrested near Quebec, on the 20th day of December, 1864, and brought back to Montreal for examination. The following are the proceedings in the Superior Court, before Justice Smith, on the demand of their extradition.*

A rare photo of former Confederate soldiers on the Canadian side of Niagara Falls, July 7, 1864. These eight men were at Niagara when the St. Albans Raid was being planned, and some were involved in attempted prison liberations at Camp Douglas and Johnson's Island. *From left to right*: Samuel E. Lackey, Louis S. Price, Squire Turner Tevis, Alamanda P. Bruce, William T. Tevis, unknown, Marcus A. Spurr and James Alexander Doty. *Photo courtesy of Ken Thomson. Published in* The St. Albans Raiders, *by Daniel S. Rush and E. Gale Pewitt.*

This time the charges were only for the personal robbery of Samuel Breck, a citizen whose $393 was stolen when he entered the St. Albans Bank.

Another round of St. Albans witnesses testified, and new witnesses for the defense took the stand. The prosecution argued that the raiders should be prosecuted in Vermont, and there was detailed discussion of jurisdiction within the United States, the government, the states, etc. Attorney Edward Sowles testified as a legal expert and stated that the raiders' robbery was a crime by Vermont law. Sowles was asked: "In your opinion, should a detachment of United States soldiers, under the command of an officer in your army, do like acts as those charged against the prisoners, your soldiers and officers being then in Georgia...would they be guilt of robbery?" After an objection by Devlin, which was overruled, Sowles responded:

I think not, Georgia is in a state of rebellion against the constituted authorities of the United States. War is going on in the state of Georgia. The Federal and so-called Confederate armies are now in the state of Georgia, and that is the battleground. The state of Vermont is not in rebellion against the authorities of the United States, but is a loyal state. Its citizens are not cimmitting [sic] acts of treason. Many of those of Georgia are so doing. I consider the act of the prisoners as an act of robbery.

Sowles stated an interesting argument basis that the prosecution was upholding. The fact that the so-called atrocities that Young and his men said they were retaliating for were being done in war zones or battleground territories such as Georgia, Virginia and the Carolinas. Vermont was not in the war zone or even close to battlefields, so the rules of war didn't apply there.

In this trial, information surfaced that the raid had been planned while the raiders were in St. Catherine's, Ontario, in August and September 1864. That caused problems with the neutrality laws since the original testimony of Young was that the raid mission had been planned on U.S. soil. The prosecution produced witnesses that attested to Young being in Toronto from the time of his escape from Camp Douglas in 1863 into 1864.

The delay tactic was used again when the Confederates' counsel, on Young's suggestion, requested a continuance for more verification and documentation from the Confederate government in Richmond. Judge Smith ordered a recess on January 10, 1865. The trial would resume on February 10, 1865.

Chapter 23

SECOND TRIAL BREAK

The U.S. government would not allow safe passage for messengers to travel through Union lines. Raiders' attorney John Houghton wrote Secretary of State William Seward, representing President Lincoln, requesting permission to pass through the lines to get to Richmond. Seward replied on January 30, 1865, that Houghton, advocate and attorney for the prisoners whose extradition in the matter of the St. Albans "murders and robberies has been demanded, is informed that the Government of the United States can hold no communication or correspondence with him on that subject. The prisoners, if they submit themselves to the authority of the United States, need no foreign mediation. So long as they remain under the protection of a foreign government, and a demand upon that Government for their delivery in the United States is pending, communications concerning them can be received only from that foreign government only through the customary channels of national intercourse."

Houghton bravely traveled to Washington and attempted to get an interview with President Lincoln, who would only agree to send him to Seward. Seward still refused the safe passage request and informed Houghton that there would be no protection if he crossed military lines or entered the rebellion territory.

A second messenger, Lieutenant S.B. Davis, traveled into the United States headed to Richmond as well. Davis was captured at Newark, Ohio, when he was recognized by paroled Andersonville prisoners. He was sent to Cincinnati, where he was tried in a military court, charged with "secretly and in disguise enter[ing] and com[ing] within the lines of the regularly organized military forces of the United States within Ohio and Michigan, with the purpose and object of going to Richmond, Va., there to deliver despatches [*sic*] and information from certain parties." Davis was sentenced to be hanged, but fortunately for him, President Lincoln sent a reprieve order, and he was instead held prisoner until the end of the war.

The danger was apparent for Confederate messengers, so the commissioners dispatched a number of them from Montreal with the hopes that some would actually make it through Union lines and get to Richmond. Especially after Lieutenant Davis's capture, it was a challenging and precarious mission they were on.

Courageously, Stephen Cameron, the chaplain, volunteered a second time to go to Richmond. He was successful and reached Richmond on February 1. He met with Secretary of State Judah Benjamin and learned that the requested documentation had already been sent by a "young woman on the day before."

Cameron, with the best interests of the Confederacy and the raiders in mind, insisted on meeting with President Jefferson Davis and procured duplicates to ensure their safe arrival in Montreal. Davis confirmed that the orders had already been sent and that they should be sufficient, but Cameron pushed until he got copies. Cameron left Richmond and returned on February 15, "bringing the certified documents bearing the great seal of the Confederacy," John Headley wrote in *Confederate Operations in Canada*.

So what happened to the documents that the female Confederate messenger had procured? And, more importantly, who *was* the "young woman?"

Headley referred to the woman as "Mrs. ——," who worked for the Confederate Secret Service and had been in Montreal at the time of the trials. Headley stated that she visited the raiders while they were incarcerated but that they had never met her before. She volunteered to run to Richmond when the need arose. Headley wrote, "After leaving the railroad in Maryland she walked much of the way through the country occupied by the enemy in Virginia. She departed from Richmond with the necessary certified papers, well concealed, one day before Rev. Mr. Cameron arrived there. These two messengers, traveling different routes, reached Montreal on the same day."

Oscar Kinchen and Headley referred to this woman as "a young widow," and Kinchen noted that she was a Kentuckian, hailing from Lieutenant Young's stomping grounds of Jessamine County. The identity of this woman has been debated. Historians James O. Hall, William Tidwell and

The St. Lawrence Hall Hotel in Montreal, Quebec (pictured here circa 1865), was located on St. James Street two blocks east of the Place d'Armes and frequented by Confederate agents, commissioners and allies during the Civil War years. John Wilkes Booth, Sarah Slater, John H. Surratt, George Sanders, John Porterfield, Clement Clay and many other well-known Confederate agents were regulars at the St. Lawrence. *Courtesy of the collections of Daniel S. Rush and E. Gale Pewitt, authors of* The St. Albans Raiders.

Kate Clifford Larson claim she was the Confederate spy Sarah Slater, aka Kate Thompson, who worked with John Harrison Surratt Jr. and John Wilkes Booth.

Sarah Antoinette Gilbert Slater was a French-speaking woman from North Carolina. She had worked with Augustus Howell, a Maryland Confederate agent and blockade-runner along the Potomac. Howell would later be implicated in the Lincoln conspirators' trial. Secretary of War James Seddon had recruited Slater, who was assigned by the Confederate Secret Service to travel to Montreal during the second trial of the St. Albans raiders. Her mission: travel to Richmond for documentation and return to Montreal. It is reported that on the way back, she traveled the regular Confederate courier routes through Virginia and met with Augustus Howell in that state and then traveled through Maryland and Washington, D.C., to New York City. Slater left Howell in New York and boarded a train to Montreal.

Slater registered at the St. Lawrence Hall, a well-known Confederate location in Montreal where all Confederate agents and associates met, on February 15. It is not clear to whom she submitted the documents, but she had completed her mission. She then left Montreal on another mission and met with John Surratt in New York. Surratt would escort her to Washington and the H Street Boarding House, the home of John's mother, Mary Surratt, who eventually would be hanged as one of the conspirators in the Lincoln assassination. Slater was involved in covert operations with Howell, George Atzerodt, John Wilkes Booth and John Surratt.

After the St. Albans raiders' trial, Slater and John H. Surratt traveled to Richmond, arriving around March 29.

By the first of April, Richmond was the next Union target, so the CSA decided to remove all the money remaining in the Confederate coffers earmarked for clandestine operations out of Canada to the safety of England. It was Sarah's responsibility to transport the money, which was mainly gold. She left the Confederate capital immediately, bound for New York City.

Some reports stated that Slater and Surratt had dispatches to deliver to Commissioner Jacob Thompson in Montreal. It was reported that she traveled through Washington, apparently alone, and visited with Booth. On April 4, Booth went to Boston and Slater to New York. It is possible that John Surratt continued on to Montreal with the dispatches, as it is believed he was in Canada at the time of the Lincoln assassination.

Neither Sarah Slater nor the money was ever seen again.

WHO WAS THE MYSTERY WOMAN?

John Headley wrote in *Confederate Operations in Canada* that he knew the female as a Kentucky woman. He noted that her name was a mystery, but a photo of her had been saved. Headley wrote that she had volunteered to help and "declined to accept from Col. Jacob Thompson any compensation whatever for her services or expenses." He reported that she was honored in 1867 at a legislation session in Frankfort, Kentucky, for her dedication.

Born Sarah Antoinette Gilbert in Connecticut to French-speaking parents, Sarah and her family relocated to North Caroline when she was a teenager. She married Rowan Slater when she was eighteen, and then he enlisted in the army and was later captured in Virginia. Rowan did return home, but Sarah was gone.

Sarah traveled to Richmond and became involved with the Confederate Secret Service. An exciting, daring new adventure began for her. She was known as the "Lady in the Veil" because of the lady's mask or veil she wore that concealed her face down to her chin. She was beautiful and mysterious, and she used her French accent and womanly charms to her advantage. With her command of the French language, Sarah could move around Canada and easily blend in. She worked with John Wilkes Booth, Augustus Howell and George Atzerodt and frequented Mary Surratt's boardinghouse in Washington, D.C. Her name surfaced many times during the Lincoln conspirators' trial and in the trial of John H. Surratt Jr. because she had spent time with John Surratt and John Wilkes Booth. Even Augustus Howell was incarcerated as a suspect in the assassination because of his connections to Booth, Surratt and Slater.

Louis J. Weichmann, a boarder at Mary Surratt's house and prosecution witness during the Lincoln conspirators' trial, provided officials with the information that Sarah was a French-speaking Confederate agent from North Carolina who carried dispatches to the Confederate organization working out of Montreal. Weichmann testified that she had visited Mary Surratt's boardinghouse about three times prior to the assassination. Slater had been seen riding in Booth's carriage in Washington.

Based on testimony given at the 1865 Lincoln conspirators' trial and again in Surratt's 1867 trial, Federal authorities were convinced Slater was the vital link that connected Booth with Richmond and Canada.

Another woman's identity surfaces in connection with the Confederate Secret Service and the St. Albans raiders documents. Olivia Floyd of Maryland served as a Confederate agent and messenger during the Civil War. It was stated that Floyd helped in getting a message from Montreal to Richmond for the request of Young's commissions. This might have been another strategy of the Confederate Secret Service, along with sending messengers from Montreal to Richmond. One way or another, the message would get through.

Floyd's story is that the "Raiders Commissions Message" was passed from agent to agent until it reached her in Maryland. Union troops were suspicious of Floyd's activities and suspected she was a secret agent. She had just received the raiders' message and decided to hide it in the hollow end of a brass andiron. The Union soldiers showed up at her door and searched the premises but couldn't find anything. After they left, she hid the message in her hair and traveled to Popes Creek, Virginia, where there was a signal station. She had the message wired to Richmond—mission completed.

After the war, Olivia's work as a Confederate agent was recognized at a Confederate reunion organized by Lieutenant Young in Louisville, Kentucky. She lived her entire life at the family home of Rose Hill in Maryland.

It doesn't seem likely that Olivia Floyd was the woman who traveled to Montreal and visited the raiders in prison or the woman who beat Cameron to Richmond to get the raiders' paperwork.

STILL IN THE NEWS

During the second trial break, newspapers covered a story about purported raiders who had escaped capture and fled Canada. The whereabouts of the rest of the St. Albans raiders were a mystery at this time, but before the Montreal trial recess, a report hit the media of five raiders in the state of New Hampshire. The following headline was printed in papers around New England, including the *Concord Monitor* in New Hampshire; the *St. Albans Messenger* on December 29, 1864; and the *Caledonian* on January 6, 1865: "The Raiders Captured at Concord." The article reported that five men attempted to enlist at the provost marshal's office at Camp Gilmore in West Lebanon, New Hampshire. Military clerk Charles Kraft, of the Fifth New Hampshire regiment, signed in the newcomers, inspected them and had them photographed.

The five men provided aliases: Frank True, Elias Atwaters, Wm. H. Cook (alias Wm. H. Brown), Henry C. Scott (alias Smith) and Henry Bowne. When Cook had his photograph taken, he commented about being one of the St. Albans raiders. When the second man, Frank True, was being photographed, Clerk Kraft said to him, "Here, you St. Albans raider, come and have your picture taken," to which the man replied, "Who said I was a St. Albans raider?" Kraft told him, and True admitted he was one of the party and had recently been released from jail. Kraft took the men to the sutler's quarters, and they ate and drank. Kraft got acquainted with the men, and they talked about themselves and their raid experiences. William Cook's wife arrived in West Lebanon soon after.

The whole party was placed under arrest by order of Major Whittlesey, and Cook's wife was searched as well, but no money other than regular bills were found in her possession. Upon being interrogated, she revealed that she was indeed one of the men's wives and that they lived in Canada before and after the raid. She stated that her husband had recently returned from Vermont with a horse and plenty of money.

It was reported that the five men had traveled northeast to Escoumains, Quebec, where they were hidden by a Canadian sympathizer. They worked their way to New Hampshire and decided to join the Union army at Camp Gilmore. If their plan worked, they would be shipped south as Union soldiers, desert and return to their Confederate units.

The newspaper article stated that the men "disclosed their plans for the future sufficient to indicate their intention to desert. Atwaters did not want to desert here, but desired to go to the front, where he intended to desert to the rebel lines the first opportunity he could obtain. Cook and Scott were anxious to desert here, and offered Kraft $700 to get them out of camp, get drunk, lose them, all of which he was ready to promise of course."

Though the men claimed they were raiders, the truth of their identities remains a mystery. They were released, and they disappeared. There was never a solid connection made with the St. Albans raiders.

Another alleged "raider caught" case is that of Hezekiah Payne, who surfaced during the second trial recess. Payne, a Kentuckian, was in the illegitimate cattle buying business with his brothers and a brother-in-law, buying Texas cattle with counterfeit Confederate money. They were indicted in Texas but escaped and made their way to Canada. Bad timing and bad connections put Hezekiah under suspicion after he had been laundering gold for John Porterfield, the Confederate financial agent. Hezekiah ended up with approximately $60,000 in stolen St. Albans notes, which he used during a poker game that was monitored by Union agents. He was lured back into the United States, arrested and extradited to Burlington, Vermont, to go on trial as a St. Albans raider. In fact, he wasn't a part of that mission, and surprisingly, he wasn't used as a scapegoat either, having been acquitted.

Chapter 24
TRIAL TWO RESUMES

The trial resumed on February 10 after the thirty-day recess. Testimony was heard from Young, Spurr, George Sanders, George Conger and various witnesses who testified that they knew the raiders. The long, drawn-out trial was monitored worldwide.

The Confederate messengers had returned from Richmond with the necessary documents. Kinchen wrote that there "was great excitement within the courtroom when it became publicly known that 'Parson Cameron' and the young Kentucky widow had at last arrived from the Confederate capital with the documents so much desired by the prisoners and their counsel."

Cameron submitted the documents he retrieved on February 15, 1865. His statement was given on that same day and entered into court records. Cameron stated:

> *Being shown and having the said papers—I say that I received them from Secretary Benjamin, Secretary of State of the Confederate States. He affixed his signature to them in my presence. I did not part with them until I handed them to the Honorable Mr. Abbott yesterday. The seal was affixed at that time—that is, the great seal of the Confederate States was affixed to them when he signed them; and he called my attention to the seal. This was in the office of the Secretary of State. I volunteered to go for the papers for the prisoners. I carried a missive from Colonel Thompson, who arranged with me about going, and supplied the funds. I called upon Mr. Benjamin about an hour after my arrival in Richmond, and he informed*

me that papers had been sent by another messenger on the day before. He said that the papers had been sent, that everything had been sent, necessary to establish their belligerent character, and that they acted under orders. The following day I called on the President, by appointment, and asked, that to ensure the safe delivery of the papers, I might be entrusted with a duplicate as a second messenger. He readily acquiesced.

Finally, on March 29, 1865, Justice Smith issued his decision, which took three hours to deliver. Smith ruled:

The attack upon St. Albans must therefore be regarded as a hostile expedition by the Confederate States against the United States and therefore an act of war and not an offense for which extradition could be claimed...They were not robbers but soldiers and subjects of a belligerent power, engaged in a hostile expedition against their enemy. Though the Confederate states are not recognized as independent, they are recognized as a belligerent power, and there can be no doubt that parties acting in their behalf would not be criminally responsible...It cannot be robbery, because open war exists between the two parties, and the law of nations does not regard as act of aggression by the subjects of the revolted country against the persons or property of the parent country as murder or robbery; it is a political or military act. I have come to the conclusion that the prisoners cannot be extradited, because I hold that what they have done does not constitute one of the offenses mentioned in the Ashburton treaty; and [thus] I have consequently no jurisdiction over them.

Lieutenant Young, Tevis, Spurr, Swagar and Bruce were discharged by the court on the grounds that they were Confederate soldiers authorized by their government to engage in expeditions against the United States. Again the crowd cheered and celebrated at the Confederates' victory in court.

The U.S. government had been informed of the discharge, and Secretary of State William Seward received a telegram from the Vermont governor dated March 29, 1865, that read: "Telegram from our consul in Montreal says raiders discharged; their acts fully sustained. Have arrested them on another warrant."

Litigation followed, and the prisoners were not released by the Superior Court until April 6. There were rumors that the prisoners would not really be released but sent to Toronto to face charges of planning there. An angry mob was outside the building and in the streets during the April 6 hearing, and rumors of rescuing the prisoners in transit and threats of violence were flying around.

Judge Smith finally ordered that the prisoners be released and their personal belongings returned to them. The celebration turned quickly to a mob commotion when Smith's release had been negated by a warrant for their re-arrest—again. It was announced that Toronto was pressing charges against the raiders. There was the threat of rioting as the raiders were preparing to be transported via train, and officials had to call in mounted artillery to line the front of the courthouse.

The trip to Toronto was safely accomplished, but must have been a sullen one.

On April 8, the *Philadelphia Inquirer* reprinted a Toronto dateline that stated, "The St. Albans robbers arrived here this morning, and were brought before the *Recorder* this afternoon, on a charge of misdemeanor, when they applied for a delay till Monday in order to obtain counsel, which was granted. They were then remanded and the case adjourned until Monday." Four days later, it was determined that Hutchinson, Tevis, Swagar and Spurr would be discharged and released. The Toronto courts would continue to hold Young. In the meantime, the Civil War had ended on April 9. Shockingly, President Lincoln was assassinated two days later.

Young was quoted in "Secret History of the St. Albans Raid," published in the *Vermonter*, as saying, "After my release at Montreal, in April, 1865, I was arrested and taken to Toronto, Canada, and charged with violating British neutrality, by organizing an armed Confederate force on Canada soil. Some noble Canadian friends became my sureties on a $20,000 bond. For ten months I demanded a trial, and at last the authorities were compelled to release me, admitting that there was no evidence whatever against me."

The trial was pending, but after the end of the war and the assassination of President Lincoln, everyone lost interest. Young was finally released in late November 1865 after a Canadian Confederate sympathizer posted his $20,000 bail.

The other raiders had been given amnesty by President Andrew Johnson and were allowed to return to the United States. Young, however, was excluded from President Johnson's amnesty proclamation and could not return home until 1868.

Chapter 25

RAID AFTERMATH

In Vermont, the frontier militia units guarded and patrolled towns and cities through the winter and into the spring. After the raiders' trials and the information about the Confederate raid plans went public, the initial panic died down.

Contrary to the rumors, the units of the Confederate military had not been sent to Canada to attack the North from the northern borders. The trials revealed that the raids were a tactic by a small group of Confederate commissioners starting with St. Albans. Since the first one created an international ordeal and shed light on the plans, the possibility of more to follow was slim.

Several provisional companies were discharged near the end of January 1865 when it was decided their presence wasn't necessary. With General Robert E. Lee's surrender on April 12, 1865, the Confederacy dissolved, and the threat of a unified presence was over. Vermonters gave a huge sigh of relief. Governor Smith disbanded the remainder of the companies on June 1.

The St. Albans Raid did provide a diversion like the Confederate commissioners had intended. It wasn't played out the way the Confederacy wanted it to be, but it did gain the full attention of Northerners and the Federal government for seven months. They had intended to have military forces sent to the northern frontier, but instead the states provided their own protection by organizing militias. It was only "diplomatic" attention that was diverted to protect an already rocky relationship with Canada and Great Britain.

The commissioners had wanted to retaliate by terrorizing unsuspecting Northern towns. That was accomplished.

Sanders had stated that one of the goals was to stir up trouble between the U.S. Federal government and the Canadian-British government. That was also accomplished. The unforeseeable aspect of violating neutrality laws was that both parties were afraid to be forced into fighting the issue. The Canadian government, on British advice, tread carefully and didn't push the issues. And the Lincoln administration was just as wary. None of the parties wanted to get into a war. The Confederate commissioners hadn't predicted that. Another surprise reaction was that Great Britain and Canada, for the most part, took into account that the entire world, not just America, was following every move of the trials. All eyes were on how the Canadians and British handled the situation.

When it was revealed that the Confederacy was indeed scheming against the Union on Canadian soil, Canadians were angry. They didn't appreciate being used as a "conspiracy" headquarters. The Canadian-British governments and the Canadian public were outraged because of the obvious neutrality abuses perpetrated by the Confederates. The attitude in Canada toward Confederates soured, and the commissioners were kicked out.

In *Raid from Hell*, Canadian Don Davison stated that the raid "created an international furor which threatened to bring Britain into the American Civil War on the side of the Confederacy. It also demonstrated to authorities in Canada and the United States of America how vulnerable the common border was." Before the St. Albans Raid, this hadn't been an issue because Canadian-U.S. relations were so strained. But after the trials and the diplomatic fiasco was averted, the Canadian-British government did not want to appear to be supporting, condoning or participating in any anti-American covert missions. And when the news of the assassination of President Lincoln hit, it didn't want to be associated with any of that either.

The future of Canada changed because of the raid. Canada had been a series of colonies under British rule but in 1868 formed its own dominion, becoming an independent entity. The St. Albans Raid might have spurred Canadians to desire authority and self-rule, a catalyst for their independence.

St. Albans's Financial Losses

For years after the raid, St. Albans tried to recover from the financial losses. Lawsuits for damages to business, personal suffering, injuries and bank losses were filed in Canada and in Great Britain.

In April 1865, the Canadian government, under direction of Lord Monck, appropriated money to be paid to the St. Albans banks. This act seemed to be a gracious, diplomatic gesture, considering that Canadian authorities, mainly Coursol and Lamothe, had returned approximately $88,000 of St. Albans money to the raiders after the first trial. The First National Bank was paid $19,000 in gold; St. Albans Bank, $20,000 in gold; and Franklin County Bank, $31,000 in original bills. These original bills had been purchased by an undercover Canadian government agent. Though the Canadian government paid these amounts, Americans were still angry about the financial loss, and Canadians were boastful that they had independently paid out of their own accounts the total loss of the St. Albans Banks when, in fact, it was just a portion.

St. Albans lawyer Henry Edson represented the St. Albans banks, and in lawsuits against the Canadian government, the three banks were able to recover more of their losses, plus interest.

The St. Albans Bank, chartered in 1853, closed its doors in 1866 after being hard hit by the raid losses. The First National Bank, which was less than a year old when the raid hit, had Hiram Bellows as bank president. Bellows was the benefactor for the Bellows Free Academy schools. First National continued until about 1883, when it closed. The Franklin County Bank, chartered in 1853, closed immediately after the raid.

Confederacy Conspiracies Revealed

As evidence came to light during the St. Albans Raid trials and, later, in the Lincoln assassination conspirators' trials, the Confederacy conspiracy plans were revealed to be devious, layered and numerous. The Northerners had no idea that schemes to undermine the Federal government were under way as early as 1862. As the war waged on and the Union was gaining the upper hand, the Confederate government chose to try covert actions to overtake the Union. The Federal government and the Lincoln administration were aware of some of these activities, but they might not have known the extent.

The St. Albans Raid was only a small part of a major conspiracy that included infecting the Northern citizens with yellow fever and smallpox, planning terrorist raids along the New England–Canada border, liberating Confederate prisoners and, worst of all, assassinating President Lincoln. The Confederate commissioners in Canada were acting on orders from President Jefferson Davis and his administration and were involved, in one way or another, with the various conspiracy operatives.

During the Lincoln conspirators' trial in 1865 and the John H. Surratt trial in 1867, the commissioners' names surfaced frequently. In Honorable John Bingham's summation at the Lincoln assassination conspiracy trial, he established the connections of the commissioners to Davis, and the common conspiracy goals of killing Lincoln were confirmed in the St. Albans Raid trials when it was established that they were working in concert. A substantial part of Bingham's summation dealt with the St. Albans Raid and these affiliations.

In fact, the raiders' trials provided valuable evidence about the Confederate commissioners that linked them to Lincoln assassin John Wilkes Booth and his conspirators: George Atzerodt, Lewis Payne, David Herold and Mary Surratt. It also implicated players from the St. Albans Raid in planning the assassination. Bingham stated:

What is the evidence, direct and circumstantial, that the accused, or either of them, together with John H. Surratt, John Wilkes Booth, Jefferson Davis, George N. Sanders, Beverley Tucker, Jacob Thompson, William C. Cleary, Clement C. Clay, George Harper and George Young, did combine, confederate, and conspire, in aid of the existing rebellion, as charged, to kill and murder, within the military department of Washington, and within the fortified and intrenched [sic] lines thereof, Abraham Lincoln, late, and at the time of the said combining, confederating, and conspiring, President of the United States of America, and Commander-in-Chief of the army and navy thereof; Andrew Johnson, Vice-President of the United States; William H. Seward, Secretary of State of the United States; and Ulysses S. Grant, Lieutenant-General of the armies thereof, and then in command, under the direction of the president?

Bingham later stated, "Who doubts that, in like manner, in the interests of the rebellion, and by the authority of Davis, these, his agents, also commissioned Bennett H. Young to commit arson, robbery, and the murder of unarmed citizens in St. Albans, Vermont?"

During this trial, revelations of the orders to Young and the use of "chemical preparations" were made public from the November 1, 1864 letter from Clement Clay to Judah Benjamin, Confederate secretary of war. It was also noted during that trial that Jefferson Davis and his subordinates had determined that "Abraham Lincoln was the deadliest enemy of the rebellion" and that throughout the Confederacy, the phrase "Abraham Lincoln must be killed" reverberated from Rebel camps in Virginia to the Andersonville war prison in Georgia to the agents in Canada. Bingham stated, "And in Canada, the accredited agents of Jefferson Davis, as early as October, 1864, and afterward, declared that 'Abraham Lincoln must be killed' if his re-election could not be prevented."

Through the trials of the Lincoln conspirators and John H. Surratt, it was apparent that a Confederate Secret Service had been conspiring against Lincoln and that Sanders, Clay, Cleary, Tucker and Thompson were involved in numerous conspiracies, not just the St. Albans Raid. Subsequently, there was a $25,000 reward for Sanders's arrest for his association with the Lincoln assassination conspirators. Jefferson Davis, former president of the Confederate States of America, was accused of treason and imprisoned at Fort Monroe, Hampton, Virginia. Never tried, he was released after two years. Clement Clay was also held at Fort Monroe on suspicion that he was involved in the Lincoln assassination plot. He was there for one year and then was allowed to return to Alabama. Sanders lived in exile for eleven years, unable to return to the States until 1876.

Epilogue

The St. Albans Raid was the northernmost land action of the War of the Rebellion. What seemed to be a random act of terror by the Confederate States of American was actually one layer in a series of covert operations to undermine President Lincoln, the Federal government and the Northern people.

However, the intricate planning of St. Albans Raid missed one major factor: the raid would be against Vermonters. Known as resilient, strong, stubborn and independent, Vermonters have always had the reputation to dig in their heels and fight if they think they are right. The Confederate commissioners and raiders did not anticipate that two posses numbering almost one hundred civilians would charge after the invaders. They thought that if they could contain the raid in one area, they would be able to scare civilians into inaction and escape unhindered.

On the contrary, civilians stood up for themselves, like Captain Conger refusing to be held hostage and breaking away from his captor to sound the alarm; or Erasmus Fuller riding into town, coming upon the raid in progress and going for his weapon to try to shoot Young; or Vermont's first lady, Ann Smith, protecting her home and family and heading down the yard with a shotgun, ready to fire at any invader coming toward her; or William Blaisdell learning the bank was in the midst of a robbery and attacking the thief.

The people of St. Albans must be remembered as heroes and heroines for their bravery, courage, tenacity and determination. Women, schoolchildren, war veterans and men at work in the banks, stores, stables, rail yard, foundry and around town all witnessed people being shot, robbed and held hostage, as well as experienced explosions, fires, Rebel yells, swearing and threats hurled at them. Their gut reaction wasn't to run and hide in the cellars until the raiders left town. No, they protected their own and chased the raiders out of town. And this applies to all Vermonters during this Confederate reign of terror. When people of the Green Mountain State received news of the raid, their immediate reaction was to grab their weapons and head to St. Albans, to the Canadian border and to Montpelier to protect the capital and their governor.

It is true that the Confederate plans to scare and terrorize Northerners worked, but the raid failed to squelch Yankee spirit. Now, 150 years after the raid, it is important to examine the whole picture and understand all the aspects involved. But, more importantly, we can renew our pride in American fighting spirit.

Appendix
BIOGRAPHIES OF VERMONTERS

GOVERNOR JOHN GREGORY SMITH

John Gregory Smith was born in St. Albans on July 22, 1818. He served in the general assembly and in the U.S. Congress. His father, Lawrence Brainerd and Joseph Clark of Milton founded the Vermont and Canada Railroad, which became the Central Vermont Railroad, and were among the originators of the North Pacific Railroad. J.G. then took over the railroad business.

In 1843, Smith married Ann Eliza Brainerd, daughter of a prominent St. Albans abolitionist and railroad associate Lawrence Brainerd. They had six children. In 1863, he was elected governor of Vermont, and he was reelected the following year. He was known as the "Soldier's Friend" for his compassion for and acts of kindness toward Vermont soldiers. He was also known as the "War Governor" because of his strong leadership during the Civil War years.

Smith handled the St. Albans Raid repercussions in October 1864 incredibly, ordering a frontier militia to protect Vermont's northern borders from further invasion. Under Smith's direction in 1864, two hundred beds were added to enlarge the hospital at Burlington, while a new hospital as Montpelier had been partially completed with accommodations for about three hundred beds.

After his gubernatorial terms, Smith was named president of Weldon National Bank, the People's Trust Company of St. Albans and the Franklin County Creamery. He donated the bronze fountain for Taylor Park and, thanks to his bequests, Smith was responsible for the construction of the library and Grand Army Hall in St. Albans.

John Gregory Smith died on November 6, 1891.

ANN BRAINERD SMITH

St. Albans native Ann Eliza Brainerd Smith was born in 1819, the daughter of Lawrence and Fidelia Brainerd. Her father was a strong abolitionist and known Underground Railroad agent. He was a partner in the railroad corporations in St. Albans with Governor Smith's father. Ann was a strong, independent woman who was accomplished as a poet, a historical novel author and a world traveler. She wrote of her experiences during the St. Albans Raid in the 1899 *Vermonter* magazine. Ann was awarded the honorary rank of brevet colonel, conferred for gallant and meritorious actions and service because of her courage during the raid. Ann died in 1905.

CAPTAIN GEORGE CONGER

Captain George Conger was born in St. Albans in 1816, one of nine children of Reuben and Sarah Conger. He was a wheelwright speculator and was also involved in the railroad business.

Conger served as a second lieutenant in the Vermont militia in 1856, serving with General George Stannard in Ransom Guard. In September 1861, he organized Company B, First Vermont Cavalry, when Vermont called for troops. He was commissioned as captain and served one year. He resigned in 1862 and returned to Vermont to care for his ill wife. He had a farm in Georgia and lived there until his later years, when he moved with his second wife to St. Albans. He married three times (Dolly Basford, Fanny Dearborn and Catherine Bliss) and had one son, George Stephen Conger.

Conger was responsible for organizing the first posse to chase the St. Albans raiders and is known as the "Hero of the Raid." He died in 1895.

MAJOR GENERAL GEORGE STANNARD

Born in Georgia, Vermont, in 1820, Stannard was one of the first Vermonters to enlist for the Civil War on April 14, 1861. He served as lieutenant colonel of the Second Vermont Infantry and colonel of Ninth Vermont Infantry and was appointed brigadier general in 1863 for bravery and distinguished valor at Harpers Ferry, Virginia.

Stannard led Vermont troops in the famous Pickett's Charge in the Battle of Gettysburg in 1863. Stannard was appointed brevet major general in October 1864 for his capture of Fort Harrison on September 29, 1864, and defeat of the enemy's efforts to retake it. It was at the Fort Harrison battle that he lost his right arm. He was home on leave when the St. Albans Raid occurred.

Stannard served as manager at the St. Albans Foundry and was later a U.S. customs collector and doorkeeper at the House of Representatives in Washington. He died there in 1889.

FARRAND STEWART STRANAHAN

Farrand Stewart Stranahan was born in New York City in 1842 and moved to St. Albans in 1859, at the age of seventeen. In the St. Albans Ransom Guard militia company, which was formed in 1856, he served with John Newton and General George Stannard.

The year the Civil War began, Stranahan married Miranda Aldis, daughter of Lawrence and Fidelia Brainerd, and they had two children. In August 1862, he enlisted in Company E, First Vermont Cavalry, serving as sergeant and then second and first lieutenant until 1864, when he was appointed aide-de-camp on the staff of General George A. Custer. Stranahan was honorably discharged in September 1864 and returned to St. Albans. He was instrumental in the response to the St. Albans event and helped John

Newton, a fellow Ransom Guard member, form a second posse to chase the fleeing raiders.

Stranahan worked as a paymaster on the Vermont Central Railroad, as a retail merchant from 1867 to 1871 and as treasurer of the National Iron and Car Company, later known as the National Car Company. He also served as a cashier and vice-president of the Weldon National Bank. He was also a director of the Central Vermont Railroad and of the Chicago, New York and Boston Refrigerator Company and was vice-president of the Missisquoi Railroad and the St. Albans Messenger Company.

Stranahan was involved in local politics before being elected to the Senate and later serving as lieutenant governor in 1888. He died in 1904.

HONORABLE JAMES DAVIS

James Davis was born in Rhode Island in 1783, and his father was a farmer and gristmill owner. Davis attended Union College in Schenectady, New York, graduating in 1809.

Davis taught at an academy in Lansingburgh, New York, and moved to St. Albans in 1810. He studied law and was admitted to the bar in 1812. Davis's first law office was in North Hero, Vermont, after which he held one in Swanton. He became law partners with Judge Asa Aldis in St. Albans in 1819.

Davis was an associate judge of Franklin County, a delegate to the Constitutional Convention and judge of probate for six years. He was an eyewitness to the St. Albans Raid and kept a diary detailing St. Albans throughout 1864 and 1865. He also wrote "Reminiscences of St. Albans by an Old Inhabitant."

WHAT BECAME OF LIEUTENANT BENNETT YOUNG?

Lieutenant Bennett Young stayed in Toronto and met and married Mattie Robinson, the daughter of a Presbyterian minister from Louisville, Kentucky, who had moved to Canada during the war. Because he could not return to

Lieutenant Bennett Young led an active, productive and successful life after he returned to the United States in 1868, becoming a historian, author, philanthropist and successful businessman. *Taken from* Confederate Wizards of the Saddle *(1914), by Bennett Young.*

the States, Young traveled to Ireland and Scotland, where he studied law and literature. He was allowed to return to the United States in 1868, at which time he settled in Louisville.

Young became one of the most prominent attorneys in Louisville. He got involved in the railroad business, contributing to the construction of the New Albany and St. Louis Railroad. A successful promoter and financier, he was involved in rail enterprise and bridge construction and was eventually was part of the Louisville Southern railway system. Kinchen noted that "the building of the Louisville Southern…is said to have been the hardest fought enterprise in Young's whole life."

In addition to being a successful businessman, Young was involved in community affairs and political ventures, serving as a consultant to young Kentucky governor J.C.W. Beckham. He was also a philanthropist, having founded the first orphanage for blacks in Louisville and the Booker T. Washington Community Center, devoted to the social welfare of black children in Louisville. He was also involved with starting a school for the blind.

History was a passion of Young's, and he wrote numerous books about archaeology, Kentucky history, prehistoric man and cavalrymen. Interestingly, he only wrote about the St. Albans Raid once, for a 1902 issue of *The Vermonter* magazine. He was a member of the Filson Club, Kentucky's oldest privately supported historical organization.

Young was the commanding major general of the Kentucky Division of the United Confederates Veterans association and was a major advocate for Confederate veterans. He traveled and spoke at many veterans association events and organized the tenth reunion of the United Confederate Veterans in 1900, held in Louisville. He was named an honorary general at the United Confederate Veterans' fiftieth reunion, held in Gettysburg, Pennsylvania, in 1913. The following year, Young was one of the keynote speakers at the Confederate monument dedication at Arlington National Cemetery.

Young traveled to Montreal in the later years of his life to visit sites that were important in his St. Albans Raid history. As for St. Albans, Young visited with St. Albans residents who were in Boston, as well as when some were in Kentucky. Young did correspond over the years with St. Albans residents George Anderson, Fuller Smith and Cyrus Bishop, who had been a cashier at the robbed St. Albans Bank.

In 1904, the planning of a raid anniversary was underway, and some residents suggested inviting Young. Some residents were still bitter, however. This was apparent in the May 1909 *Boston Transcript*, which ran an article about Young not being welcome in St. Albans for a tercentenary celebration: "Ex-Governor Ormsbee of Vermont has fired what is probably the last shot at General Bennett H. Young of Kentucky, as the latter withdraws from all participation in the Champlain Tercentenary celebration." The article reports that the organizing committee invited him but that area veterans' organizations protested:

> *Union veterans headed by ex-Governor Ormsbee protested that while they could forgive and forget much, they held Young and his raiders unforgiveable...The invitation had the aspect of a commercial proposition devised to attract the attendance of those curious to see the leader of the*

St. Albans raid. There is a certain kind of forgiveness that smacks of sycophancy, and we fear that it is not entirely absent from some occasions for fraternizing the Blue and the Gray.

Young's last major project was to help create the Jefferson Davis monument that stands in Fairview, Kentucky. It was under construction at the time of Young's death in 1919.

BIBLIOGRAPHY

Adams, H.K. *The St. Albans Raid: Investigation by the Police Committee of the City Council of Montreal into Charges Preferred by Councillor B. Devlin.* Montreal: Owler & Stevenson, 1864.

Andrews, Roland Franklyn. "How 'Unpreparedness' Undid St. Albans." *The Outlook* 114 (1912).

Bailey, Thomas A. *A Diplomatic History of the American People.* New York: Appleton-Century-Crofts Inc., 1958.

Benjamin, L.N., comp. *The St. Albans Raid; or, Investigation into the Charges Against Lieut. Bennett H. Young and Command, for Their Acts at St. Albans, Vt., on the 19th October, 1864.* Montreal: J. Lovell, 1865.

Benton, Rueben C. "Personal Recollections of the St. Albans Raid of 1864." *Glimpses of the Nation's Struggle.* Vol. 3. New York: D.D. Merrill and Company, 1893.

Borthwick, J. Douglas. *History of the Montreal Prison, from A.D. 1784 to A.D. 1886.* Montreal: A. Periard, 1886.

Branch, John, et al. *St. Albans Raid, October 19, 1864.* St. Albans, VT: St. Albans Historical Society, 2001.

Branch, John, Sr. *Reminiscences at the Publishing of the First Raid Booklet.* St. Albans, VT, 1935.

Childs, Hamilton. *Gazetteer and Business Directory of Franklin and Grand Isle Counties, VT, for 1882–83.* St. Albans, VT, 1883.

Clark, Gerald. "When Southern Raiders Rode over the Border." *The Standard,* June 15, 1940.

Clay-Copton, Virginia. *A Belle of the Fifties: Memoirs of Mrs. Clay, of Alabama.* New York: Doubleday, Page & Company, 1905.

Coffin, Howard. *Full Duty: Vermonters in the Civil War.* Woodstock, VT: Countryman Press Inc., 1993.

Crockett, Walter Hill. *Vermont: The Green Mountain State.* Vol. 3. New York: Century History Co., 1921.

Cross, Helen. *The Green and Gold of 1928 Yearbook.* (Contains Cora Burgess's and James Record's letters about the St. Albans Raid). St. Albans, VT, 1928.

Dowden, Albert Ricker. "John Gregory Smith." *Vermont History Journal* 32, no. 2 (April 1964).

Goodman, Lee Dana. *Vermont Saints and Sinners.* Shelburne, VT: New England Press, 1985.

Headley, John Williams. *Confederate Operations in Canada and New York.* New York: Neale, 1906.

Hemenway, Abigail. "Raid of '64." *Vermont Historical Gazetteer.* Vol. 2. N.d.

Hill, Reverend Howard. "The St. Albans Raid." *The Vermonter* 5, no. 1 (August 1899).

Holbrook, Stewart. "Confederates in Vermont." *Man's Magazine* 18, no. 107 (April 1946).

Jampoler, Andrew C.A. *The Last Lincoln Conspirator: John Surratt's Flight from the Gallows*. Annapolis, MD: Naval Institute Press, 2008.

Johnson, Carl E. *The St. Albans Raid: 19 October 1864*. St. Albans, VT, 2001.

Kauffman, Michael W. *American Brutus: John Wilkes Booth and the Lincoln Conspiracies*. New York: Random House, 2004.

Kinchen, Oscar A. *Daredevils of the Confederate Army: The Story of the St. Albans Raiders*. Boston: Christopher Publishing House, 1959.

————. *General Bennett H. Young: Confederate Raider and a Man of Many Adventures*. Boston: Christopher Publishing House, 1981.

Larson, Kate Clifford. *The Assassin's Accomplice: Mary Surratt and the Plot to Kill Abraham Lincoln*. New York: Basic Books, 2008.

Long, E.B. *The Civil War Day by Day: An Almanac, 1861–1865*. Garden City, NY: Doubleday & Company, 1971.

Lutz, Stuart. "Terror in St. Albans." *Civil War Times*, June 2001.

Marshall, Jeffrey D. *A War of the People: Vermont Civil War Letters*. Hanover, NH: University Press of New England, 1999.

Mellinger, Edward D. "Rebel Raiders in Vermont." *Tradition* 3, no. 1 (December 1960): 48–57.

Morrison, Leonard Allison. *The History of the Morison or Morrison Family*. N.p.: A. Williams and Company, 1880.

Pitman, Benjamin, comp. *The Assassination of President Lincoln and the Trial of the Conspirators*. New York: Moore, Wilstach & Boldwin, 1865.

Possons, Charles H. *Advantages, Resources and Attractions of St. Albans, VT*. St. Albans, VT: St. Albans Board of Trade, 1889.

Pritchard, Russ A., Jr. *Raiders of the Civil War: Untold Stories of Actions Behind the Lines*. Guilford, CT: Globe Pequot Press, 2005.

Robinson, Philip G. *The Town Under the Cliff: A History of Fairlee, Vermont.* Fairlee, VT: Fletcher Printing, 1996.

Rush, Daniel S., and Gale E. Pewitt. *The St. Albans Raiders.* Chatham, VA: Blue and Gray Education Society, 2008.

Sherman, Michael, Gene Sessions and Jeffery P. Potash. *Freedom and Unity: A History of Vermont.* Barre, VT: Vermont Historical Society, 2004.

Smith, Mrs. J. Gregory. "An Incident of the Civil War." *The Vermonter* 4, no. 6 (January 1899).

————. "An Incident of the Civil War, Concluded." *The Vermonter* 4, no. 7 (February 1899).

Sowles, Edward. *A History of the St. Albans Raid, Annual Address Before the VHS, October 17, 1876.* St. Albans, VT: Messenger Printing Works, 1876.

Squires, Melinda. "The Controversial Career of George Nicholas Sanders." Master's thesis, Western Kentucky University, 2000.

St. Albans Historical Museum. "Personal Observations of the St. Albans Raid." *Local History* 5 (Summer 1997).

————. *The St. Albans Historical Museum History Walk.* St. Albans, VT: Messenger Print & Design, n.d.

St. Albans Historical Museum, L. Louise Haynes and Charlotte Pedersen. *Images of America: St. Albans.* Charleston, SC: Arcadia Publishing, 2010.

St. Albans Historical Society. *St. Albans, Vermont, through the Years 1763–1963: A Bicentennial History.* Edited by Margaret B. Armstrong, Pamela J. Caldwell and Dorothy C. Steele. St. Albans, VT: St. Albans Historical Society, 2008.

Steers, Edward Jr. *The Lincoln Assassination Encyclopedia.* New York: Harper Perennial, 2010.

Tidwell, William A. *April '65: Confederate Covert Action in the American Civil War.* Kent, OH: Kent State University Press, 1995.

Tidwell, William A., James O. Hall and David Winfred Gaddy. *Come Retribution: The Confederate Secret Service and the Assassination of Lincoln.* Jackson: University Press of Mississippi, 1988.

Trindal, Elizabeth S. *Mary Surratt: An American Tragedy.* Gretna, LA: Pelican Publishing, 1996.

Walsh, James. *Story of St. Albans Raid, October 19, 1864.* St. Albans, VT: Reprinted from the *St. Albans Daily Messenger*, 1939.

Wells, Frederic, and Edward Miller. *History of Ryegate, Vermont.* St. Johnsbury, VT: Caledonian Company, 1913.

Winkler, H. Donald. *Stealing Secrets.* Nashville, TN: Cumberland House, 2010.

Woodard, Jon. "The St. Albans Raid: Rebels in Vermont!" *Blue & Gray Magazine* 8 (December 1990).

Young, Bennett Henderson. *Confederate Wizards of the Saddle.* Boston: Chapple Publishing Co., 1914.

———. "Secret History of the St. Albans Raid." *The Vermonter,* January 1902.

SPECIAL COLLECTIONS

Musee McCord Museum, Montreal, Quebec.

St. Albans Historical Society and Museum Collections, St. Albans, VT.

University of Vermont Special Collections, Bailey-Howe Library, Burlington, VT. Andrew Craig Fletcher to Andrew and Ruth Fletcher, October 20, 1864, and November 2, 1864. Consuelo Northrop Bailey Papers, Carton 063, Folder 006, Item 011.

Vermont Historical Society Leahy Library, Barre, VT. Documents, articles, photos, John Branch souvenirs of St. Albans Raid box, Frank Greene files.

Vermont State Archives Collection, Waterbury, VT. Repository for Vermont state military, legislative and court records.

WEBSITES

hernandoheckler.wordpress.com
labarregalleries.blogspot.com
revdsmackay.wikidot.com
www.canadachannel.ca
www.civilwarsoldier.com
www.collectionscanada.ca
www.csacurrency.com
www.findagrave.com
www.ironbrigadier.com
www.lostcause.com
www.old-maps.com
www.sonofthesouth.net
www.stalbansraid.com
www.wtv-zone.com

ARCHIVE SOURCES

Blue and Gray Education Society, Chatham, VA (Leonard Riedel)
The *Caledonian* archives
Documenting the American South website and archives
Frank Leslie Illustrated Weekly archives
Harper's Weekly archives (www.sonofthesouth.net)
National Archives (files, images, documents)
New York Times archives online (www.nytimes.com)

Personal collections of Daniel S. Rush, E. Gale Pewitt, Wayne Mitchell, Donald Miner, Earl D. Goldsmith, Ken Thomson, Robert Eldridge and Michelle Arnosky Sherburne.

The *St. Albans Messenger* archives

Vermont Department of Libraries

www.Fold3.com

www.newspapers.com (national newspaper archives)

Index